MINNESOTA DRAMA
EDITIONS

Founding Editor: Sir Tyrone Guthrie
Series Editor: Michael Langham
Advisory Board:

MINNESOTA DRAMA EDITIONS NO. 9

MINNESOTA SHOWCASE: FOUR PLAYS

★★★★★★★★★★★★★★★★★★★★★★★★★★★★★★★★★★★

Introduction
by Michael Langham

Do Not Pass Go by Charles M. Nolte

Georg Büchner's *Woyzeck,* adapted by David Ball

Fables Here and Then by David Feldshuh
and the Guthrie Theater company

The Cookie Jar by John Clark Donahue

★★★★★★★★★★★★★★★★★★★★★★★★★★★★★★★★★★★

With comments by Charles M. Nolte, David Ball,
David Feldshuh, and Linda Walsh Jenkins

MINNEAPOLIS • THE UNIVERSITY OF MINNESOTA PRESS
in Association with The Guthrie Theater

Foreword

The four theater pieces in this book indicate that theater activity — professional or amateur — can nurture the creation of many types of viable experiences. At any given time, there are between twenty-five and forty producing groups in Minneapolis and St. Paul. Much of their work is predictably inadequate, but even inadequate work can serve as a necessary training ground for young theater artists, and the practical theater experience is more valuable to them than any classes could be. The aspiring writer, director, actor, or designer must be free to fail — even miserably. There are few places outside the Twin Cities where someone can do this and yet be given a second, third, even fourth chance. In the Twin Cities one need not dazzle with the personal debut. There is a milieu here in which a young artist's work can be viewed time after time, so that someone with real talent can learn — through doing, through erring — how to offer it.

The four pieces in this volume represent some of the finest work being done by Minnesota playwrights, and they certainly display the enterprise that this area generates. *Do Not Pass Go* is one of many plays written by Charles Nolte, whose work is given frequent local staging. David Ball's adaptation of *Woyzeck*, a kind of work too formidable to be performed often, found a home at two different local theaters. *Fables Here and Then*, created by David Feldshuh and produced by The Guthrie Theater, toured the Upper Midwest and met with exultant responses everywhere. And John

Donahue's *The Cookie Jar* is an example of many fine works created by him and his Children's Theatre Company of the Minneapolis Society of Fine Arts, a theater that has attracted international attention.

Charles Nolte received his early training at the University of Minnesota. In the midst of a successful career as a Broadway actor (playing, for example, the title part in *Billy Budd*) he rejected Broadway because of its stifling penchant for typecasting and returned to the university to teach. He began writing plays from an actor's perspective and experience. He wrote roles for actors to do — and even in his less successful plays the challenge to actors is remarkable. At one point Nolte was criticized in a playwriting class for limiting his writing to well-worn forms. His response was the unconventional *Do Not Pass Go.* The play has since been done in New York (with Nolte in one of the leads), it has been seen on National Educational Television, and it has received productions in many parts of the world.

David Ball is a good example of one who has seized the opportunities open to playwrights in the Twin Cities. In the past four years he has had no fewer than thirty-five productions of his work, a number inconceivable for even an established playwright anywhere else. With David Feldshuh he adapted the Guthrie versions of *An Italian Straw Hat* and *A Christmas Carol,* and he has recently received a Tyrone Guthrie Award to support his research for the writing of a play based on Minnesota history. In his various scripts he utilizes a wide variety of forms and styles as he seeks to combine structured theatricality and respect for the spoken word. Plays by both Ball and Nolte have received production grants from the Office for Advanced Drama Research at the University of Minnesota, an organization dedicated to discovering new playwrights; the O.A.D.R. is directed by Arthur H. Ballet and is funded by the Rockefeller Foundation.

David Feldshuh joined the Guthrie in 1968 as a McKnight Fellow in Acting from the University of Minnesota, and in 1972 he became an associate director of the company. *Fables Here and Then* was created in large part by young members of the Guthrie acting company during rehearsal under Feldshuh's vigorous direction. They started with a method and a theme, and slowly, through discussion and improvisation, they evolved a script from stories, anecdotes, and newspaper items. *Fables* represents a kind of theater where words are secondary to movement, mime, sound, and technique. Feldshuh's background in mime, his skill in theater games, and his training in karate were exploited to create a vividly choreographed production. He worked with the idea that any detail not absolutely essential to telling the story should be cut — and in about eighty minutes the piece explores as much content as there is in many full-length plays. *Fables* developed a widespread new audience for the Guthrie and has since been reproduced at other professional theaters.

John Donahue is a director of remarkable vision. He wrote and directed *The Cookie Jar* at his Children's Theatre Company of the Minneapolis Society of Fine Arts, a theater that owes its fame and success primarily to his genius. Donahue's work does not fit the prototype that defines most of the last fifty years of children's theater in America: it does not condescend, it is not "easy." Donahue does not pass off lesser work because "only" children are watching; he believes that no play for children is adequate unless it is good for adults as well. In the space of a few years he has built a theater organization that can display acting, directing, writing, and designing of the finest quality. While his staff continually searches for new plays, almost all of the works done in the past years have been developed in his theater, most often following a scenario by the director which is subsequently bodied forth in rehearsals. Donahue's achievements are too numerous to summarize here, but a significant one has been to attract thousands of children as regular theatergoers — children who in the future may become an avid and unusually sophisticated new audience for adult theater. *The Cookie Jar* is an example of the demands Donahue makes upon his audiences. And his audiences respond. Parents do not accompany their children simply to babysit; they go to see the plays for themselves.

If *Do Not Pass Go, Woyzeck, Fables Here and Then,* and *The Cookie Jar* are good plays — and I think they are — their greatest importance lies in their promise. And they are part of a broad undercurrent of serious theater writing in Minnesota that shows signs of erupting sooner or later into something that would be exceptional anywhere.

Michael Langham

Contents

Minnesota Showcase: Four Plays

Do Not Pass Go

(a play in one act for two actors)

Charles M. Nolte

Comments

Shortly before the first production of *Do Not Pass Go* at the Cherry Lane Theater in New York in the spring of 1965, the director Alan Schneider wrote asking for any thoughts I wished to express before he began rehearsals. My response, paraphrased in part below, was a long and rambling letter which touched on many aspects of the play: the naturalistic format, its atmosphere of Grand Guignol, the various psychological factors motivating the characters, and not unnaturally my own trepidation. Could we retain audience interest over a whole evening with two characters in the stock room of a run-down Los Angeles supermarket?

Mr. Schneider particularly wanted to know what *I* thought the play as a whole was all about, and I responded:

> . . . many things, but perhaps essentially about the conflict between youth and age which I feel to be a paramount aspect of our society today. The young man Crawford speaks of a new form of "racism," the war between young and old. "Stay young, stay with it," he cries, "that's the real race war, between young and old." In a society where age is accorded no real dignity, the message is clear on every hand. Old people are hidden from view in "leisure worlds" and other retirement concentration camps. Some of course do not attain even this fate. Alone and penniless, old Lewis is not equal to the struggle. He is a useless piece of human garbage, and Crawford has definite ideas about what to do with these misfits who clutter up the scene. Are Crawford and Lewis then merely symbols of youth and age? By no means are

5

they as simplistic as that. Crawford has many of the evils of modern society in general clustering to his image, and Lewis is surely not "average." Both are more than symbols, each with a definitely reconstructible past behind him.

The play becomes the dramatization of a terrible struggle carried out in a series of sadistic games where the odds are stacked. You do not realize until the very end that it has been a final struggle and the games in deadly earnest. But what Crawford does to Lewis in the final minutes of the play must seem, after it is over, to have been inevitable given his character and the situation. I don't think he can be viewed as simply another delinquent. His approach to life is more cerebral and articulate than that.

Also obvious in the play is a comment on modern society as a society of things, of rampant materialism. The stock room itself with its mass of consumer goods stacked floor to ceiling is the metaphor: Wild Canadian Blueberry Syrup and Uncle Ben Rice, Chili Pronto and Toitoi Tissue in Vanity Pink. Surrounded by this abundance and doubtless hypnotized by advertising, being part of the generation raised on TV, Crawford spends days humming commercials and mindlessly repeating empty slogans drummed into his ears. He has a poet's appreciation for the styles and rhythms employed by the ad agency boys. A car is never simply a car to him, it is always a Chevy Monza with spoke wheels or a Mustang Hardtop with a breezy little sunroof and competition suspension. He isn't content to simply say "ice cream." It must be Lady Diana Coffee Spin or six quarts of Fruit Caprice. This is his language, sly, paradoxical, filled with a peculiar imagery and weighted with cynicism, a language which Lewis, who is of an older and more reticent generation, finds alien and threatening.

But like many in his own generation, Crawford instinctively senses the fraudulent nature of his society and its language. His way with a phrase suggests ironic awareness of the shabbiness of the American dream, and there is an echo of bitterness in much of his talk.

Poor Lewis, on the other hand, clinging precariously to a minimal existence and erupting now and then into pure paranoia, speaks in a kind of mangled, elliptical prose which suggests his sense of outrage at life which he cannot control and in fact no longer even understands.

A short time after writing my thoughts to Alan Schneider, events turned out in such a way that I found myself in New York rehearsing the role of Crawford for the premiere. Since that time, I have seen the play in Frankfurt, London, and Berlin, as well as in several American cities, and have myself directed it in Minneapolis. I recognize that it usually has limited audience appeal, but I feel that it reflects aspects of modern American society in a persuasive form, if one is prepared to be open-minded.

Charles M. Nolte

Do Not Pass Go

Characters

Crawford

Lewis

Setting

The crowded stock room of a run-down Superette in a shabby beach area of Los Angeles, in Venice or Pacific Ocean Park. Crates of canned goods, dry cereals, and boxes of all kinds are stacked to the ceiling. Sacks of potatoes and other produce are piled at the rear near a corrugated metal door which opens onto an outside loading platform. Attached to a pillar in the center of the room is a squawk box used to communicate with the main part of the store. At one side there is a locker for clothes and near it a sink and a small cupboard faced with a mirror. On the other side a thick door with a small glass aperture opens into the cold-storage room. On the opposite side swinging doors lead into the store. There is a worktable at the center with rubber stampers, odd boxes, and crates. Overhanging light fixtures with green shades give the dank and crowded room a garish atmosphere. The action passes without interruption on the day before Christmas.

At rise, Crawford stands at the sink combing his hair before the mirror. He is an energetic young man in his twenties with a likable and ingenuous nature, a kind of Billy Budd innocence and openness of face. His long hair is wheat-colored, bleached by sea and sun. He wears faded dungarees and a clean white apron; his well-developed chest and arms are emphasized by a formfitting T-shirt. He has a heavy signet ring on one hand. A black eyepatch covers his left eye. When he moves, it is with lithe and effortless grace. He finishes combing his hair, whistling softly to himself, and removes a small mirror from his pocket and glances at his profile. He hears a noise off, looks toward the door leading into the store, then steps quietly out of sight behind a stack of cardboard boxes as Lewis backs through the door and into the room. Lewis is a confused old man of seventy, grizzled and worn by hardship and poverty. He is dressed in faded work pants and a dirty gray shirt. Upset and angered, he makes threatening gestures with his broom and looks balefully toward the swinging doors and the store beyond. Hidden in the shadows Crawford meows softly like a cat. Lewis freezes, listening intently. Crawford emerges and crosses nonchalantly to the sink where he begins washing his hands. Lewis turns toward him.

LEWIS
 You hear a cat?
CRAWFORD
 What's that, Lewis?

LEWIS

You hear a cat just now?

CRAWFORD

A cat?

LEWIS

Thought I heard a cat.

CRAWFORD

(*meticulously washing his hands*) No, I didn't hear any cat, Lewis.

LEWIS

(*approaching him, his voice rising angrily*) Say, you know what that Peterson says to me? First thing he tells me, bring in a crate of lettuce, see . . . An' then he says, right outa the blue, when you gonna get a haircut, Lewis. When you gonna get a haircut!

CRAWFORD

Peterson said that?

LEWIS

(*vehemently*) Told me to get a haircut.

CRAWFORD

(*drying his hands with deliberation*) But you don't need a haircut, Lewis. You got a fine head of hair.

LEWIS

(*with disgust*) Well, what the hell . . .

CRAWFORD

You couldn't shoot a bullet through that hair.

LEWIS

Haircut, fer crissake!

CRAWFORD

(*eyeing Lewis appraisingly*) Where you going, Lewis?

LEWIS

Huh?

CRAWFORD

You been invited somewhere? Is that it? (*Lewis blinks uncomprehendingly.*) Somewhere you didn't tell your old buddy? Gonna pay your respects to that preacher down in

Lynwood? Has that preacher friend invited you over for Christmas dinner or something?

LEWIS

What the hell you talking about?

CRAWFORD

(*as if to a child*) Where you going that you need this haircut?

LEWIS

I ain't goin' nowheres!

CRAWFORD

Then why do you need a haircut?

LEWIS

(*explosively*) I don't need no goddam haircut, fer crissake, that's what I'm tryin' to tell ya! (*turning away in disgust*) Ahh, what the hell. No sense talkin' to you. I shoulda known that by now.

CRAWFORD

Complain to your union, Lewis. Say you don't want a haircut. (*He begins stacking crates, moving with muscular grace.*) A haircut would be wasted on you.

LEWIS

No man can tell me get a haircut. No man's got that right. I got rights same as that Peterson.

CRAWFORD

No question about that, Lewis.

LEWIS

(*muttering*) Damn winos anyway, the whole bunch of 'em.

CRAWFORD

Who's a wino, Lewis?

LEWIS

Why, them barbers. Winos, the whole bunch of 'em. (*following Crawford as he works*) Listen, lemme tell ya, I had this barber once, see. An' he had me sittin' there, in this barber chair . . .

CRAWFORD

(*quietly*) Hands, Lewis.

LEWIS

Now listen a minute, will ya . . . ?

CRAWFORD

Remember what I told you.

LEWIS

He had me sittin' up there in this chair, see, lookin' at myself in this mirr' . . . I was sittin' there with this big mirr' right in front a my face . . .

CRAWFORD

(*softly*) Hands . . .

LEWIS

They had it fixed so's you couldn't look nowheres else. Had that mirr' rigged so's you had to look right at it.

CRAWFORD

Just a minute, Lewis.

LEWIS

(*going on*) An' he had me sittin' there, see . . .

CRAWFORD

Your hands.

LEWIS

(*exasperated*) Hands! Hands! What about my hands, fer crissake!

CRAWFORD

The lilywhites are gliding around in front of you like a couple of big white birds. Now, Lewis, I'm carrying you in medium-close and your hands are going right out of frame. Can't you tie 'em down, strap 'em to your legs or something?

LEWIS

(*blinking*) Wha-a-t?

CRAWFORD

(*patiently*) I want to concentrate on what you're saying, and the lilywhites are going right out of frame. (*Lewis stares at him uncomprehendingly. The voice of Peterson is heard coming over the squawk box, loud and scratchy.*)

VOICE

Crawford!

CRAWFORD

(*stepping to the box and depressing the lever*) Yes sir, Mr. Peterson.

VOICE
   Uncle Ben Rice.

CRAWFORD
   (*making a note on a pad next to the box*) Uncle Ben Rice.

VOICE
   Case of Chili Pronto.

CRAWFORD
   Chili Pronto, yes sir.

VOICE
   Say, we got any of that Wild Canadian Blueberry Syrup?

CRAWFORD
   Will check.

VOICE
   You got that old fart working?

CRAWFORD
   Lewis, sir? Oh yes, Lewis is very busy back here.

VOICE
   Well, where in hell is my iceberg lettuce! Don't let him stand
   around all day with his thumb up his butt.

CRAWFORD
   No sir, wouldn't think of doing that.

VOICE
   And move up a couple crates of Florida seedless.

CRAWFORD
   Will do. (*turning to Lewis*) Hear that, Lewbaby? Mr. Clark W.
   Peterson wants to know where's that lettuce you promised him.

LEWIS
   (*muttering sourly*) An' then you know what he done?

CRAWFORD
   Peterson?

LEWIS
   No, not Peterson, fer crissake, this barber I was tellin' you
   about.

CRAWFORD
   (*assembling the items Peterson asked for*) What did he do?

LEWIS

When he was done givin' me this cut, see, he takes down this other mirr' an' shows me the back a my head.

CRAWFORD

Pretty strange, if you ask me, showing a man the back of his own head.

LEWIS

(*positively*) I tell you he took down this mirr' an' showed me the back a my head!

CRAWFORD

Guess what, Lewis. I went to Fat Eddie's on Pico this morning all set to have a stack of wheats. Only guess what I saw. Cat tracks in the pancake batter.

LEWIS

Wha-a-t?

CRAWFORD

No kidding. There were cat tracks in the pancake batter again this morning. Little paw prints. Now what do you make of that?

LEWIS

(*struggling to understand, then blurting*) Only it wasn't me, see.

CRAWFORD

What wasn't you?

LEWIS

Sittin' there in that barber chair, that wasn't me. That was some other guy sittin' there. They done that with a trick a the mirr', see . . .

CRAWFORD

(*at the squawk box, depressing the lever*) Mr. Peterson . . .

LEWIS

(*positively*) I tell you that wasn't me sittin' there. I know the back a my own head, fer crissake. You think I don't know the back a my own head?

CRAWFORD

(*shaking his head sadly*) I don't know, Lewis . . .

LEWIS
I tell you that wasn't me sittin' there . . .

VOICE
(*on the squawk box*) Yeah?

CRAWFORD
Definite negative on that Canadian syrup, sir. Want me to list it?

VOICE
Gimme six dozen.

CRAWFORD
Check. Coming right up with the Florida seedless.

LEWIS
(*as Crawford turns toward him*) I know the back a my own head, fer crissake. Don't I know the back a my own head?!

CRAWFORD
You got a real problem here, Lewis. (*He moves off to get a crate of oranges.*)

LEWIS
(*sullenly mumbling to himself, feeling his scalp tenderly*) Damn winos anyway, standin' there like some kinda doctors or somethin', all dressed in white . . .

CRAWFORD
What makes you think doctors wear white?

LEWIS
I ain't talkin' about doctors, I'm talkin' about them wino barbers!

CRAWFORD
Your smart surgeon turns up in a nice shade of lime green these days, Lewis. With matching face mask.

LEWIS
Who the hell they think they are, fussin' round the eyes with them sharp scissors? (*fiercely, his voice rising*) How'd you like it if some damn wino barber was fussin' round your eyes with a sharp pair a scissors . . . ? (*Crawford turns slowly to stare at Lewis. A wave of fear sweeps over Lewis. His face goes white. A pause, then Lewis smiles cravenly and speaks in a whining voice.*) I dint mean

that, Crawford. It just slipped out. I dint mean nothin', honest to God . . .

CRAWFORD

(*in a low, sad voice*) When you're searching for a relationship, Lewis, you don't go around stirring up the waters. You don't up-set the old applecart. Because two can play that game. What if I were to mention Welch Grape Juice, for instance? Would you break out in a blotchy rash? Would your voice go all constricted?

LEWIS

(*cringingly*) But I dint mean nothin', see. Honest to God, it just slipped out.

CRAWFORD

I'm gonna let it pass this time, Lewis, but I'm afraid your grade went way down. (*He takes a note pad from his pocket and makes a notation.*) Afraid you only get a C-minus, Lewbaby, only a C-minus on this Haircut Bit. You know why? Not enough comic relief. No laughs, Lewis. And then that unfortunate slip at the end, when you mentioned scissors around the eyes.

LEWIS

What you puttin' down there?!

CRAWFORD

"Lewis Sopko, the Haircut Bit, C-minus."

LEWIS

Say, what is this, school or somethin'? You got no right to grade me!

CRAWFORD

(*pocketing the note pad*) It's performance that counts, Lewis. We're all graded.

LEWIS

You got no call to grade me! This ain't no school, fer crissake!

CRAWFORD

(*hoisting a crate to his shoulder*) C-minus, afraid that's the best I can do. (*He goes to the door, exits.*)

LEWIS

(*shouting after him*) You got no call to grade me . . . (*muttering to himself as he begins sweeping with desultory motions*) Damn winos . . . Never met a barber yet wasn't a wino . . . Like havin' an operation, fer crissake, gettin' a haircut. Worse. When you have an operation they got ya drugged so's you don't feel them sharp scissors . . . (*glancing apprehensively toward the door*) You think them barbers'd use drugs on you? Ssss, not on yer life they wouldn't! I got sensitive hair. (*defiantly*) I got sensitive hair! I feel every cut . . . (*muttering softly*) Damn winos anyway . . . (*Crawford bursts into the room juggling three grapefruit. He tosses them at Lewis in rapid succession. Lewis scrambles after them.*)

CRAWFORD

Rejects, Lewbaby. Compliments of Mr. Clark W. Peterson. He's out there prodding fruit again. Ever watch him? The way he takes up a grapefruit, prods and pinches it, sniffs at it? Now, could you pass such a test, Lewis? If Peterson treated you the way he treats grapefruit, checked you out for lice and long hair and varicose veins, could you pass such a test?

LEWIS

(*defiantly*) I do my job, sonny!

CRAWFORD

Like that iceberg lettuce you were supposed to bring out?

LEWIS

Oh Jesus, I forgot.

CRAWFORD

Seems you did.

LEWIS

Did he wanna know where that lettuce was at?

CRAWFORD

I covered for you, buddy. I got my buddy's problems in mind.

LEWIS

You dint say I was loafin' on the job or nothin', did ya?

CRAWFORD

Now, would I say a thing like that?

LEWIS

He's got it in fer me, I know that fer a fact. That Peterson, he hates my guts. Hell, you think I don't know why? Cuz he hadda gimme this job, that's why. That preacher told him to gimme this job. I got friends! I don't depend on that Peterson, not by a long shot.

CRAWFORD

(*at the door, looking off into the store*) There he is now, going into Poultry. Nope, he's turning back. He's in Frozen Foods, checking the Birds Eye TV dinners and Eskimo Fishsticks . . . (*turning back to Lewis*) How about a quick game of "blink," Lewbaby? Shall we have one quick game of "blink" while Mr. Peterson dainties up the fishsticks?

LEWIS

You gonna cheat again? (*Crawford looks at him reproachfully.*) I dint mean that, Crawford, honest to God I dint.

CRAWFORD

(*smiling brightly*) No, I like that, Lewis. Wonderful change of mood, and that little chuckle, that really saved the scene. Well, do you wanna play or don't you?

LEWIS

(*enthusiastically*) Sure, sure!

CRAWFORD

Okay, one quick game of "blink" while Mr. Clark W. Peterson tippytoes through the Birds Eye. Now remember, one blink is all you get but everything you see during that blink belongs to you. Those are the rules.

LEWIS

(*excitedly*) Do I get to wear the gunnysack too?

CRAWFORD

Of course you wear the gunnysack. Now on your mark, get set . . . (*Lewis hunches over, his eyes tightly closed.*) Keep those eyes closed till I give the word. Ready . . . Blink! (*Lewis straightens up and stares wildly around the room for a long second. Crawford takes a gunnysack and places it over Lewis's head so that he cannot see. During the next few speeches, Crawford swiftly and quietly eases a crate marked "Welch Grape Juice" into the center of the room, then takes a dish of cream from the locker and places it on the floor.*) Boom! Man oh man, Lewis, you took a real man-size blink there! Wow, that was some blink! Where'd you learn to blink like that?

LEWIS

(*trembling with excitement*) Wait, wait now . . .

CRAWFORD

Oh baby, what a blink. Did you blink like that back home when you were a kid?

LEWIS

Naw, we never even played "blink" when I was a kid.

CRAWFORD

You never played "blink"? Well, whaddya know. All right, GO, man!!

LEWIS

Now lemme think, don't rush me . . . (*stabbing the air with his finger*) Aha! Them crates a oranges.

CRAWFORD

(*sitting with a note pad and a pencil*) Crates of oranges.

LEWIS

An' them boxes Swansdown.

CRAWFORD

Check.

LEWIS

Lettuce on the floor there, by yer feet.

CRAWFORD

You want those dead leaves, Lewis?

LEWIS

Whacha mean, do I want 'em? Ain't that part a the game? I seen 'em, dint I?

CRAWFORD

Give that man his rotten lettuce.

LEWIS

(*slyly*) Strawberries . . .

CRAWFORD

I challenge that. Where'd you see any strawberries?

LEWIS

Never mind where I seen 'em.

CRAWFORD

Now who's cheating, Lewis?

LEWIS

(*triumphantly*) Eggs!

CRAWFORD

Where?

LEWIS

There, stacked up by the wall, them Grade A Browns.

CRAWFORD

Very good, Lewis. Check that stack of Grade A Browns.

LEWIS

Now wait, wait, don't rush me, lemme think . . . Aha, case a cling peaches! Big case a clings.

CRAWFORD

Check.

LEWIS

(*chuckling*) I knew they was some clings somewheres. An' them sacks a potatoes, whole slew a them sacks over there, all belong to me.

CRAWFORD

I give 'em to you, Lewis. Take all that pulp, as far as I'm concerned.

LEWIS

Yer damn right.

CRAWFORD

You done?

LEWIS

(*angrily*) What the hell you mean, done! Course I ain't done. Not by a long shot. How about that door on the coldbox?

CRAWFORD

(*patiently*) You want that door, Lewis?

LEWIS

(*vigorously*) An' that little window with the thick glass, all that's mine. I seen it.

CRAWFORD
Nobody denies that, Lewis.

LEWIS
An' what about them boxes a soap there?

CRAWFORD
(*kicking a box*) This Fairy Snow?

LEWIS
Yer damn right.

CRAWFORD
With New Blue Whitener?

LEWIS
An' them Cocopops too, that stack a Cocopops.

CRAWFORD
You claiming all that?

LEWIS
Yer damn right I am.

CRAWFORD
Give this man his Cocopops. Give this man his Fairy Snow with New Blue Whitener. That all?

LEWIS
Wait, wait now. I ain't done yet. (*feverishly*) Ain't there some big cartons a toilet paper by the door there? Dint I see some toilet paper there?

CRAWFORD
This Luxury Twinpac Toitoi Tissue in Vanity Pink? That what you mean?

LEWIS
Yeah.

CRAWFORD
A very practical man.

LEWIS
I fooled you on them eggs, dint I?

CRAWFORD
Yes, Lewis, you really had me fooled on those Grade A Browns.

LEWIS
    Yer damn right.

CRAWFORD
    Yes sir, cling peaches, Cocopops, Toitoi Tissue in Vanity Pink, all that Fairy Snow with New Blue Whitener, all belongs to you.

LEWIS
    An' that coldbox door with the little window, don't forget that.

CRAWFORD
    All yours.

LEWIS
    Yer damn right. Them are the rules. (*Lewis submits as Crawford removes the gunnysack from his head. Lewis looks around feverishly, like an excited child at play.*) I done real good, heh, Crawford?

CRAWFORD
    Not too bad, Lewis, all things considered.

LEWIS
    I like playin' that game, that's a real good game.

CRAWFORD
    (*folding the gunnysack*) But think what you missed, Lewis.

LEWIS
    Huh?

CRAWFORD
    What you missed.

LEWIS
    What'd I miss?

CRAWFORD
    You really want me to tell you? No, it only spoils the game.

LEWIS
    (*grabbing him*) What the hell'd I miss, fer crissake? What was so important I missed? (*Crawford smiles enigmatically.*) You mean I missed somethin' real special.

CRAWFORD
    Um-hum.

LEWIS

Like what, fer crissake!

CRAWFORD

(*softly*) Like that car heading west on Venice.

LEWIS

What car!

CRAWFORD

(*blandly*) Powder blue Mustang.

LEWIS

Where?

CRAWFORD

Out that window.

LEWIS

I dint see no car.

CRAWFORD

While you were staring around with your eyes popping out, right out that window. Powder blue Mustang with balloon tires, heading west on Venice.

LEWIS

(*anguished*) Wasn't no car out there.

CRAWFORD

And you know who was driving that car? There was a girl behind the wheel of that thing, and I tell you she was a real doll, Lewis. Wearing this cute little blouse real tight across the tits. Beehive hairdo. Big wet lips. Soft puddle of baby fat under the chin. Man oh man, that girl was just on the turn, Lewbaby, she was IT. Wouldn't surprise me if that girl was some starlet under contract at Universal. Some cute broad they're grooming for big things. And she woulda been your slave for life, Lewis. Cuz those are the rules.

LEWIS

(*suspiciously*) You sure you seen a car?

CRAWFORD

Now, would I kid about a thing like that? (*Lewis turns away, bitterly disappointed.*) But let's forget that powder blue Mustang and go over what you *did* see. First, that little item: one coldbox.

LEWIS

(*defensively*) That's mine!

CRAWFORD

No, Lewis, only that door is yours.

LEWIS

(*hotly*) I seen it!

CRAWFORD

(*quietly*) Nobody denies that, Lewbaby, nobody says you didn't see that door. But I guess you forgot to look inside that coldbox.

LEWIS

(*crushed*) Oh Jesus, I forgot again.

CRAWFORD

Guess you did. Guess you failed to see that carton of ice cream in there.

LEWIS

(*pained*) Ice cream?

CRAWFORD

Lady Diana Coffee Spin.

LEWIS

In there?

CRAWFORD

That's right. In plain sight.

LEWIS

(*piteously*) Ain't no Coffee Spin in there, is there?

CRAWFORD

(*drawing him toward the glass window*) Now you tell me what you see. What's that box there? What's it say?

LEWIS

(*miserably*) Oh Jesus . . .

CRAWFORD

And look there, Lewis. Lemon Twist.

LEWIS

Jesus . . .

CRAWFORD

You know what else is in there? Six quarts of Fruit Caprice. That coldbox is loaded, Lewis. All that ice cream sitting in there at two below just waiting to be claimed. Only you screwed up again. You were so busy scooping dead lettuce off the floor you missed the Coffee Spin. Now there's a lesson in that, Lewbaby. What is that lesson? (*pause*) You don't know what that lesson is? Well, I'm gonna tell you. The lesson is, Lewis, you're a crumb. That's right. (*sadly, with compassion*) I said to myself the first time I walked in here and saw you leaning on a broom, I said, now there's an old crumb if I ever saw one. (*tenderly, with gentleness*) And you know something else? It's your own fault. You made yourself a crumb because you were the first person who believed it . . .

LEWIS

Esther . . .

CRAWFORD

No, not Esther, you.

LEWIS

(*breaking down*) You got no right treatin' me this way. When Esther was here nobody said them things to me.

CRAWFORD

But Esther isn't here any more, baby, and that's what we got to face. (*Lewis sinks to his knees, his lips working convulsively. Crawford bends down and holds him in his arms, speaking soothingly.*) I'm only trying to help you, baby. Believe me. You know what Mr. Peterson told me the first day I came to work here? Old Lewis back there, he said, see if you can't keep him busy. Cuz otherwise we got to send him up to Camarillo, and I hate to do that . . .

LEWIS

(*weeping*) You got no call sayin' that. I ain't goin' up to that place. I do my job.

CRAWFORD

Hey now, don't start bawling on me. That's no way for a grown man to act. (*gently cradling him*) When we start bawling, we're just going backwards. And I thought we'd made better progress than that. I thought I'd shown you how to strip away all that self-pity. That's what's dragging you down, baby, and you got to fight it. You got to chuckle at the little setbacks. You gotta laugh when the going gets tough. Why, you were doing real great last week, remember? You even laughed out loud when you told me the Grape Juice Bit, remember?

LEWIS

Uh-huh . . .

CRAWFORD

Well then . . . (*gently raising him*) Now come on, baby. We'll go over it carefully from the beginning.

LEWIS

I don't wanna play no more, really, Crawford . . .

CRAWFORD

But you got to, Lewis. You gotta play the game, cuz that's the way things are . . . (*Crawford wipes Lewis's face with his handkerchief.*) There we are, Lewbaby, all fixed up again. (*Crawford turns away from Lewis and walks to the sink with an anguished expression. He tosses his handkerchief into the corner, brushes his arms and chest where his body has been in contact with Lewis's. During the next few speeches he washes and dries his hands with meticulous thoroughness.*) Now. What else did you miss, Lewis? (*silence*) What else did you miss while you were so busy scooping dead lettuce off the floor? (*Lewis stares dumbly.*) Lewis?

LEWIS

I dint see nothin' else, honest to God, Crawford . . .

CRAWFORD

Nothing? (*simply*) Not even that case of Welch Grape Juice?

LEWIS

(*tensely*) Where?

CRAWFORD

Right in front of you.

LEWIS

(*stepping back in panic as he sees it*) Where'd that come from?

CRAWFORD

You mean to tell me you didn't see that case of Welch staring you in the face? Where are your eyes, Lewis?

LEWIS

(*staring at the case, confused and frightened*) Wasn't there before . . .

CRAWFORD

(*matter-of-factly*) And of course you saw that cat.

LEWIS

Cat?

CRAWFORD

Right down there by those boxes.

LEWIS

What cat?!

CRAWFORD

Funny. I could've sworn you saw that little ginger cat peeking out with his tail in the air, sniffing at that little dish of cream. Why, look, see, there's his little dish of cream . . . (*Peterson's voice is heard on the squawk box, suddenly loud and raucous.*)

VOICE

Crawford.

CRAWFORD

(*at the box*) Yes sir, Mr. Peterson.

VOICE

Running low on homogenized.

CRAWFORD

Coming right up, sir. (*Crawford crosses to the coldbox, pulls open the heavy double door, and enters. Lewis begins searching for the cat, stumbling desperately among the crates and boxes.*)

LEWIS

Kitty . . . Kitty . . . Where's that cat gone . . . ? Here, kitty kitty . . . Hey, listen, Crawford, there wasn't really no cat here, was there . . . ? Kitty kitty . . . You back there, goddammit

. . . ? Kitty kitty . . . Ain't no cat here, I know that . . .

CRAWFORD

(*emerging from the coldbox balancing a case of milk on his shoulder*) Fat-free milk, fat-free milk, one-a-penny, two-a-penny, fat-free milk . . .

LEWIS

(*whimpering*) Listen here, Crawford . . .

CRAWFORD

Cold in there, baby. (*going toward the store*) Où sont les neiges d'antan, Lewis? Answer me that and you win a year's supply of Puss'n Boots. (*He exits into the store.*)

LEWIS

(*calling after him*) Crawford . . . You dint really see my cat back here, did ya? (*turning away*) Ahh, what the hell's he talkin' about? He was only kiddin' me. Always playin' games, that young punk. All alike, these kids today. Sons a bitches, ain't got no respect at all . . . Wasn't no cat here, I know that fer a fact . . . That cat is gone. Ain't never comin' back . . . (*muttering sourly*) Who sent the niggers downtown, fer crissake. How the hell should I know who sent the niggers downtown . . . (*Muttering angrily to himself, he glances down at the carton of grape juice, then quickly looks toward the door to see if he has been observed. He begins to scrutinize the carton carefully. He opens the lid and slowly extracts a bottle of grape juice, looking at it apprehensively and holding it to the light. Crawford enters behind him, stands silently watching him, a smile on his lips.*)

CRAWFORD

(*whispering*) I see you . . .

LEWIS

(*whirling in confusion*) Oh Jesus . . . (*Desperately he works to replace the bottle of grape juice.*)

CRAWFORD

(*crossing swiftly to Lewis, putting on a pair of dark glasses, his personality subtly changing, becoming aggressive*) Gimme a Number Twenty lens and a couple of baby spots right here. This man's got a statement to make. Two baby spots and six feet of track. I wanna go from a tight two-shot into full-screen closeup for this.

LEWIS

Wasn't no cat, was there, Crawford . . .

CRAWFORD

(*kneeling by Lewis, speaking intimately*) Now here's what we're gonna do, Lewbaby. This is your big scene. I'm going into full-screen closeup for it . . .

LEWIS

Listen, Crawford . . .

CRAWFORD

You got the lights. The pink gels all in place. (*shouting offstage*) Kill the blowers! Gimme the arcs! I want quiet!

LEWIS

Crawford . . .

CRAWFORD

(*shouting*) QUIET! (*silence*) Okay, roll 'em . . . (*He kneels near Lewis and speaks low.*) Now I put the question to you, Lewis, in all seriousness. Why didn't you bring that case of Welch Grape Juice into the store?

LEWIS

(*baffled*) Wha-a-t?

CRAWFORD

(*low, tense*) Why didn't you bring out that case of Welch?

LEWIS

(*plaintively*) Listen here, Crawford, you dint . . .

CRAWFORD

(*hard*) I'm waiting, Lewis.

LEWIS

No, really — listen, Crawford . . .

CRAWFORD

(*growing angry*) Now don't louse me up, baby. I'm wasting film. Why didn't you bring that Welch into the store like I told you to?

LEWIS

You dint tell me nothin' like that . . .

CRAWFORD

(*shouting angrily as he rises*) Cut! Cut cut cut!! God Almighty, Lewis, we went all over these lines before. You had 'em cold.

LEWIS

(*blinking, confused*) What the hell you talkin' about?

CRAWFORD

I get my lights set up, I bring in six feet of track, I dolly in close. And what happens? You louse me up. You got any idea the trouble you cause by withholding that Welch? Do you realize there are ladies out there, good suburban housewives stocking up for the long Christmas weekend, wondering what in hell has happened to the Welch Grape Juice? Those good ladies are waiting, Lewis, lined up all the way out to the checkout counters, standing four deep back of the Bubble-Ups. They're fighting out there, tearing up the cornflakes, throwing chips all over the place. Women are going mad out there, dying for Welch Grape Juice . . .

LEWIS

(*suddenly shouting*) Listen to me, fer crissake! (*Immediate silence. Crawford rises abruptly and crosses to the sink removing his dark glasses. He begins to wash his hands methodically. Lewis shouts wildly.*) What's goin' on here?! Games, all the time playin' some crazy games. Well, I ain't playin' no more, you hear? You nuts or somethin'? Welch Grape Juice! Don't you tell me nothin' about Welch Grape Juice, you hear!

CRAWFORD

(*hanging up his towel with neatness, then turning to Lewis, speaking in a tired voice, slowly shaking his head*) I been very patient with you, Lewis. Very patient. But you got to remember I'm keeping score. (*He takes out his note pad and makes a notation.*) Another C-minus, Lewis. Afraid that's the best I can do. You know why? Know why you only get a C-minus on this Welch Grape Juice Bit? You didn't laugh once. Not once. And you know what that is, Lewis? That's just refusal to grow up. We got to face our little problems in life, Lewis. We have to be adult. You're no kid, you know. So be adult. (*with a bright, encouraging smile*)

Now, what was it you wanted to say to me? (*Pause; Lewis blinks uncertainly.*) You had something to say about Welch Grape Juice. Just take it easy and tell me calmly.

LEWIS

(*baffled*) Wha-a-t?

CRAWFORD

You had something you wanted to say. Well, what? I'm listening, Lewis . . . Nothing to say?

LEWIS

(*explosively*) I got plenty to say!

CRAWFORD

(*softly*) All right, then . . . (*He smiles beatifically.*)

LEWIS

(*with sudden fierceness*) They never know when to quit, that's the trouble!

CRAWFORD

Who, Lewis?

LEWIS

(*with disgust*) Why, them barbers.

CRAWFORD

Back to the barbers, are we?

LEWIS

(*aggressively*) Damn winos. Always askin' questions. They don't just cut the hair, no. They all the time got to ask you some damn question. You want this stuff on yer hair? You want me to slosh on this shampoo stuff? Fer crissake. I tell you, when I go to this barber, they got me sittin' up there starin' at a whole shelf full a bottles and jars and stuff . . .

CRAWFORD

(*blandly*) So?

LEWIS

(*with baffled anger*) Well, what the hell! They got me starin' at this whole shelf full a stuff an' some damn wino asks me, you want some coal tar on yer hair? Fer crissake!

CRAWFORD
>   Coal tar?

LEWIS
>   Some damn coal tar stuff. As if I ain't got enough on my mind
>   without some damn wino barber puttin' coal tar on my head. You
>   got any idea how hard it is gettin' tar outa yer hair?!

VOICE
>   (*on the squawk box*) Crawford!

CRAWFORD
>   (*at the box*) Yes sir, Mr. Peterson.

VOICE
>   Hustle out some Aunt Mary Albertas.

CRAWFORD
>   Right.

LEWIS
>   That tar don't come out easy. You gotta get that out with
>   kerosene, fer crissake. But what the hell do you do, I'd like to
>   know. Yer trapped in that damn barber chair, trapped, that's all.

CRAWFORD
>   (*picking up a basket of peaches*) I got the solution, Lewis.

LEWIS
>   (*snorting*) You got the solution! What solution, fer crissake?

CRAWFORD
>   Very simple, Lewis. You just leave. Get up and go. (*He exits into
>   the store.*)

LEWIS
>   (*shouting after him*) Just get up and go, huh? How the hell you
>   gonna do that, fer crissake? You think you can go running down
>   the street with a barber sheet round yer neck? You think they'll let
>   you get away with a thing like that? (*Blinking with outrage, Lewis
>   sinks down to the floor, muttering to himself. During the next few
>   lines he takes out his lunch bag, extracts a soggy doughnut, and
>   begins to munch on it.*) Why, first thing you know, some fat cop'll
>   grab at you and ask you why the hell yer runnin' down the street
>   with a sheet round yer neck. Whatcha say when some fat cop asks

you that, I'd like to know. What the hell you say to him, runnin' down the street with some damn sheet round yer neck? He's liable to say yer nuts or somethin'. He's liable to send you up to Camarillo, fer crissake . . . (*eating stoically*) Damn winos anyway . . . (*pause*) That cat ain't comin' back . . . Ain't never comin' back. I know that fer a fact . . . (*He stares out, his jaws working slowly. Crawford enters carrying a movie fan magazine which he leafs through as he speaks.*)

CRAWFORD

Lemme tell you about Life, Lewbaby. It's a two-shot, see. My old man sitting at the dining table in a cloud of Union Leader. Now get this, Lewis. I come into frame just home from junior high. Cradling an armful of books. Little skinny kid with pimples. My old man looks up, frowns at me, and bites down on his pipestem. Hell, you can see the muscles grind into a ball on his jaw. Can't you carry your books like a man? he says. Do you gotta go round like some kind of hermaphrodite? Now we cut to my room upstairs. I'm back of the door with this dictionary open in my hands. We move in on my face. I feel puzzled and sick. Hell, I'm only fifteen, Lewis. That's a very impressionable age. Okay, Lewis, you get the picture? Now fade to black, and then it's a low angle on this big York barbell, two hundred, two-twenty pounds. We pull back, and there I am, shoulders out to here, seventeen-inch upper arms. Get the picture? That's all it takes, Lewb. A little hint, and POW! I gotta hand it to my old man. Now I walk like a man, arms down at my sides. I don't hide behind the furniture . . . (*Pause; he looks at Lewis, who continues eating stolidly.*) I get the feeling you haven't heard a word I've said . . . What you thinking, Lewbaby? I can hear you thinking way over here, trying to squeeze some little thought out your brain.

LEWIS

(*with disgust*) Why, this damn wino barber, he wanted to pop my skull.

CRAWFORD

Pop your skull?

LEWIS

Pop my skull, fer crissake.

CRAWFORD

Now just a minute, Lewis. You can't say a thing like that right outa the blue. You gotta gimme a voice level before making a statement like that. (*making a megaphone out of the fan magazine and calling offstage*) Bring in your boom. Gimme a level here. Man's got a statement to make. (*To Lewis*) Now, Lewis, slowly and distinctly, so all the folks can hear. What's all this about popping your skull?

LEWIS

Why, this damn wino barber, when he was through cuttin' my hair, he says to me, I wanna pop yer skull. That's a helluva thing to say to a man. I wanna pop yer skull! Wake up all them dead hairs, he says. Put the blood back in them folly-cules. Well, what the hell. I says to him, I says, listen, don't worry none about them folly-cules. You just cut the hair, I told him, you just cut the hair!

CRAWFORD

(*rolling over, clutching his sides, laughing silently*) Holy man, that's great, Lewbaby, that's real great. A definite B-plus on this skull-popping routine. (*calling out*) Hey, poppers of the skull, unite! You got nothing to lose but your folly-cules!

LEWIS

(*sourly*) Damn winos anyway, the whole bunch of 'em.

CRAWFORD

Man oh man, that's a real great scene, Lewbaby, that skull-popping routine.

LEWIS

(*muttering*) Who says I got dead hairs anyway? Who the hell says that . . .

CRAWFORD

(*looking at the magazine*) Lewis, will you tell me . . . in all seriousness now, let's cut the crap . . . You think Shirley Temple will ever reveal what she and Jane Withers used to do behind the steam tables in the Fox commissary?

LEWIS

(*muttering*) Winos, all of 'em . . .

CRAWFORD

You're not much help, Lewis. You're just not much help. (*Lewis chews in silence. Crawford leafs through his magazine. A pause.*) Is that your stomach I hear, Lewis? (*Lewis turns away, continuing to eat.*) Animal, that's all you are, animal at the trough. Everybody should eat in separate rooms, with the food shoveled in through a hole in the wall. If there's anything I hate, it's the sound of chewing. Know what that reminds me of? Sitting at breakfast back home. My old man grinding toast on his molars. Nobody saying a word, not one word. I had to get up and turn on the news to drown out that sound. Just the sound of people chewing killed my appetite. People are cattle. That's all they are, cattle. Well, what do you know. Tiny Tim refused point-blank to be on the cover of *Your Physique*. I just don't know what the world's coming to. I'm getting one hell of a feedback, Lewis. Your stomach is rumbling and I'm getting one hell of a feedback. It's lousing up my sound track. You got no teeth. That's why your stomach rumbles that way.

LEWIS

I got teeth, sonny. Don't you worry none. I got teeth.

CRAWFORD

Oh, you got teeth, all right. I see you take 'em out and wash 'em in the sink.

LEWIS

(*shocked*) No.

CRAWFORD

You deny that?

LEWIS

When'd I ever do a thing like that?

CRAWFORD

You deny you slip out that plate and give it a rinse after you eat?

LEWIS

Ain't none a yer business what I do.

CRAWFORD
Makes me physically sick to see a grown man take out his teeth and rinse 'em off like that. I'm gonna hide those teeth on you one of these days. Then you'll have to go on mechanical soft.

LEWIS
What's 'at you say?

CRAWFORD
I'll put you on mechanical soft, that's what I'll do.

LEWIS
(*bristling*) Nobody puttin' me on mechanal soft, I'll tell you that right now.

CRAWFORD
Yes sir, you proceed this way, I'm afraid I'll have to put you on mech-an-i-cal soft. Because I'm getting a heavy feedback and it's killing my appetite.

LEWIS
(*defiantly*) Just what the hell's that, mechanal soft?

CRAWFORD
(*sweetly*) Very simple. They just put it all through this big stainless steel machine. Thirty or forty times it goes through, and comes out sort of muddy brown. All pre-chewed. Yes sir, if you don't stop that rumble, I'm afraid I'll have to pin a little white diet card to your shirt. And every noon they'll come round with a rubber tube and squirt the mechanical soft into your mouth like a baby.

LEWIS
Ain't nobody puttin' me on mechanal soft, I'll tell ya that right now!

CRAWFORD
Why so touchy, Lewboy?

LEWIS
(*hotly*) You hear! I ain't goin' on no mechanal soft!

CRAWFORD
But I'll be there to help, baby. I'll put the bib on so's you don't dribble and smear all over your face the way they do up at Camarillo.

LEWIS

Huh? What's 'at you say about Camarillo?

CRAWFORD

That's where they invented the mechanical soft. And that's where you'll end up if you can't control that little rumble. You might just end up at Camarillo if you live that long.

LEWIS

I'll live, sonny. Don't you worry none about me. I'll live to beat the cars. And I ain't goin' up to no bughouse at Camarillo. (*rising defiantly*) Nobody gonna put me in that bughouse. I know all about that place. I got rights. That fella down to Lynwood, that preacher friend a mine, he's got my intrists to heart. He's thinkin' a me all the time. Why, dint he come over when Esther went like that? Dint he get me this job here? No sir, sonny, that preacher ain't gonna let nobody take me up to Camarillo, I'll tell ya that right now. All I gotta do is get on the phone, he'll be right over.

CRAWFORD

Well, I'll be a son of a gun. Lovely Ava Gardner was seen on Sunset Boulevard in broad daylight wearing woman's attire.

LEWIS

(*digging at his wallet*) I got rights! Look there! See that? That there's my social security card. I got rights.

CRAWFORD

How about that, Lewis. In broad daylight.

LEWIS

Ahh, what the hell . . . (*He subsides, returns to his lunch bag.*)

CRAWFORD

You suppose it's really true, Lewbaby, that Natalie Wood is gonna inherit all of Paul Muni's old roles at Warners'?

LEWIS

I can't help that rumble. A man my age can't help it . . . (*He withdraws a small package from his lunch bag, glances to see if Crawford is watching, then carefully unwraps it.*)

CRAWFORD

(*quietly, without looking up from his magazine*) What you got there, Lewis?

LEWIS
(*flustered*) Huh? Why, nothin' . . .

CRAWFORD
Why you hiding it, then?

LEWIS
I ain't hidin' nothin'.

CRAWFORD
What is it? Lemme see.

LEWIS
I told you, nothin'.

CRAWFORD
Give it here. Gimme that thing, Lewis. (*taking the package*) What is this, some new kind of dessert or something?

LEWIS
(*reaching for it*) Give it back.

CRAWFORD
Now just a minute, don't get so grabby. You said it was nothing. If it's nothing, how come you want it so bad?

LEWIS
It's mine.

CRAWFORD
I'm not gonna eat it, Lewis. I'm not gonna eat your precious dessert. I just want to ascertain what it is makes your stomach rumble that way. (*peering skeptically at the label*) Now, what is this thing we got here? (*reading portentously*) "Banana Pretty. A barquette of pastry filled with banana, cream, and nuts, all covered with flaky chocolate . . ." Well, I'll be a son of a bitch. This is a Banana Pretty! All covered with flaky chocolate. How about that. Where'd you get this, Lewis?

LEWIS
Never mind where. I bought that.

CRAWFORD
You bought this Banana Pretty? Where?

LEWIS
Reiffenburger's.

CRAWFORD

Oh, you did, did you? You stepped into Reiffenburger's Bakery and purchased this Banana Pretty, is that it?

LEWIS

(*reaching for it*) Now gimme that.

CRAWFORD

Don't be so greedy.

LEWIS

Come on, Crawford . . .

CRAWFORD

This your dessert, Lewis? You mean to tell me, on top of all that stale bread and soggy doughnuts you were planning to gobble this Banana Pretty?

LEWIS

(*reaching*) Please . . .

CRAWFORD

Just a taste, Lewis. Just one bite. That's all I want. (*Lewis watches miserably as Crawford takes a generous bite and chews appraisingly.*) This isn't for you, Lewis. You'll get sick eating this thing.

LEWIS

(*miserably*) Crawford . . .

CRAWFORD

(*another bite, chewing meticulously*) This is nothing for an old man to eat. It'll make you toss your cookies sure as a gun.

LEWIS

Won't make me sick. I never been sick, never sick a day. Doctors gimme a clean bill just last summer.

CRAWFORD

This thing is enough to drive a dog off a gut wagon. Did you feed this to your cat? Is that what did it? That cat of yours finally quit home because you dosed him with Banana Pretty? I'd hate to see your insides, Lewis. All this Banana Pretty sliding down your tubes, you'll end up with a coronary big as a butcher's thumb. (*He squeezes the remaining Banana Pretty into a pulp and throws it into the trash basket, smiling brightly at Lewis.*)

LEWIS

Now, why'd you go do that?

CRAWFORD

What?

LEWIS

Throw away my Banana Pretty . . .

CRAWFORD

I did that to save your life, Lewis. I saved you from eating that poisonous thing and that's all the thanks I get. It's bad enough watching you gum your way through a soggy doughnut, but I draw the line at Banana Pretties. That's where I positively draw the line. (*He is at the sink, washing his hands.*)

LEWIS

I been lookin' forward to that all mornin' . . .

CRAWFORD

(*quietly, with sincerity*) I hated to do that, Lewis, I really did. But I just had to. I love my buddy too much to let him eat crap like that.

LEWIS

I dint give no Banana Pretty to my cat, Crawford. Honest to God, I never done a thing like that.

CRAWFORD

I know that, Lewis. I was just teasing.

LEWIS

That cat wouldn't a touched one a them things with a ten-foot pole.

CRAWFORD

(*gazing at himself in the mirror*) I showered this morning with a brand-new cake of Pink Dove, Lewbaby. I'm head over heels in Pink Dove. (*With a grotesque insuck of breath he strikes a pose, flexing his muscles.*) Ever see a lat spread like that? The thing about this T-shirt, Lewis, it really grips you. Hugs the old pecs, leaving you completely free as you bali-hi the Florida grapefruit. Yes sir, this formfit is alert. Clean cut. It's got swagger, a man's kind of snugness.

LEWIS

About that stomach rumble, I can't help that none . . .

CRAWFORD

(*posing*) Lookit that arm, Lewis.

LEWIS

A man my age can't help that none.

CRAWFORD

Isn't this color a dream? It's voodoo blue. I'm a dream chorale in voodoo blue. The thing is, Lewis, your formfit comes in a variety of shades. Nile green, banker's gray, shell pink. But my very favorite is golden cognac.

LEWIS

You dint mean that about mechanal soft, did ya?

CRAWFORD

I tell you, Lewis, when I stop out on Robertson in my golden cognax with a pair of white Levi's stenciled to my thigh . . .

LEWIS

Ahh, what the hell . . .

CRAWFORD

Think young, Lewis. Eat your yogurt and think young. Do that, you got it made.

LEWIS

(*angrily*) You young punks, you think ya own the world, doncha? Sons a bitches . . .

CRAWFORD

All kidding aside, Lewb, is it really true Shelley Winters was seen pricing whips at the Farmers' Market?

LEWIS

You got no call scarin' hell outa me that way, you got no call, ya hear?!

CRAWFORD

(*moving toward the exit*) Back to our cabbages, old buddy before Mr. Clark W. Peterson has a hemorrhage. Hey, it's the middle of the afternoon, Lewis. And we still haven't had a single run-through on the Esther Grape Juice Bit.

LEWIS

    Ahh, fer crissake . . .

CRAWFORD

    (*exiting into the store*) Get on the stick and run your lines.

LEWIS

    (*glaring after him*) I can't help that rumble none . . . Ahh . . . Don't know what's comin' next with this punk. All the time playin' games. I gotta get down to Lynwood, that's all. Gotta tell 'em they're fixin' to ship me up to Camarillo. That preacher'll sure as hell tell 'em where to head in . . . (*An idea glimmers in Lewis's brain. He looks off to make sure he is alone, then fumbles in his pocket and draws out a crumpled cigarette. He looks at it avariciously, puts the stub in his mouth, takes a packet of matches from his pocket, and strikes a light. At that moment Crawford reenters. In a frenzy Lewis waves out the match, removes the cigarette, and stuffs it into his pocket.*)

CRAWFORD

    (*waving a gaudy Christmas card*) Lookee here, Lewis, bet you can't guess what this is.

LEWIS

    (*much flustered*) Whatcha got there?

CRAWFORD

    This is the Clark W. Peterson family Christmas card, just this minute handed me by Mr. Peterson himself. Yes sir, Lewis, this is the Peterson family card. See there, you got the whole family. Mama, Papa, and all the little Petersons. The whole family. Lookit Mrs. Peterson. Catch the nose on that woman. You ever see a nose like that before? Why, I bet if that woman sneezed real hard her upper plate would come sailing out that nose. What do you bet? Now look here, Lewis, you open this up and inside you find this chatty newsletter. See, the year's activity in a nutshell. (*reading*) "Another year gone. Mike is Honor Roll at senior high. Star scout, devoted to sports, peanut butter, and the girl next door." How about that, Lewis. Peanut butter! "Dave is a tenth-grader now. His dad's gonna make a halfback outa him ..."

Look at that little pinched-up face. That kid'll never live to see seventeen. He'll perish under the arcs on the thirty-five-yard line, vomiting Welch Grape Juice in the last quarter of the homecoming game. Well, there you are, Lewis, the Peterson family card. All the little Petersons may advance directly to GO and collect their two hundred. (*coldly*) But you, Lewis, you do not pass go.

LEWIS

Huh?

CRAWFORD

You were trying to sneak a smoke on me, weren't you? And that's ·against the rules.

LEWIS

Me smoke? (*fawningly*) You know I wouldn't do a thing like that, Crawford . . .

CRAWFORD

What the hell's that in your pocket?

LEWIS

What?

CRAWFORD

(*digging savagely into Lewis's pocket*) This! What the hell you doing? Working on a carcinoma? Is that what you want?

LEWIS

(*weakly*) Well, what ya know . . .

CRAWFORD

You got any other weeds on you?

LEWIS

Honest to God . . .

CRAWFORD

(*with intense feeling*) You know the history of this cancer stick? You know what's in this thing? All that crap sucking into your lungs . . . (*He grinds the cigarette in his fist.*) No wonder you're old and stupid and sick, gotta have something sticking in your mouth all the time. What a filthy habit. Be clean, Lewis! Don't suck all that dirt into your lungs. Be clean!

LEWIS

(*cringingly*) I dint mean to do it, honest to God . . .

CRAWFORD

(*crossing to the sink and washing his hands*) The body, that's all you got, Lewis. Keep it clean. (*Breathing heavily, Crawford rinses his hands with fussy thoroughness as Lewis stands uncertainly, watching him.*)

LEWIS

(*finally*) I dint mean to do it, Crawford. I just forgot . . .

CRAWFORD

I got half a mind to go out there and report you to Mr. Clark W. Peterson.

LEWIS

(*fawningly*) Naw, you wouldn't do that, would you, Crawford?

CRAWFORD

You really disappoint me, Lewis.

LEWIS

I won't never do it again, honest to God . . . Hey, you wanna hear about Esther like you said? I'll tell you about Esther now. Would you like that?

CRAWFORD

No. I don't want to hear about Esther. I'm really sore. I mean it. (*Crawford folds his towel carefully and hangs it up. Then in a sudden change of mood he turns to Lewis with a winning smile.*) Well, old buddy, we gonna hear about Esther today? How about it, Lewbaby? The Esther Grape Juice Bit?

LEWIS

(*confused*) But you just said you dint wanna hear . . .

CRAWFORD

You misunderstand, Lewis. I'm trying to impress that story on my mind. That's one of the great stories of our time, the Esther Grape Juice Bit. I never tire of hearing you tell it.

LEWIS

(*sulkily*) Well, I ain't in the mood now.

CRAWFORD

Don't fight me, baby. You're fighting me.

LEWIS

You gonna tell about yer eye then?

CRAWFORD

Have I ever disappointed you?

LEWIS

Promise?

CRAWFORD

Come on, baby. The old Mitchell's on a dolly, we're moving in slow. I'm cutting to a Number Twenty lens, holding you close. Now just remember, keep it light, keep it gay. A little ripple of laughter, a couple of chuckles in the right places, makes all the difference . . .

LEWIS

(*haltingly*) Well . . . Lemme see . . . this was, this happened . . . I ferget just when . . .

CRAWFORD

(*low, tense*) We're rolling, baby. Come on, the boom is moving in.

LEWIS

This was in the bedroom, see . . .

CRAWFORD

All the facts, baby. Whose bedroom?

LEWIS

Esther's. Only I was up already, see. I been up two, three hours already. Had my coffee and grits. An' I went in there, see . . . into the bedroom to see why dint Esther get up like she always done . . . (*a little self-conscious giggle*) An' she was lyin' there, see . . .

CRAWFORD

(*murmuring*) Oh, great, great . . .

LEWIS

With her teeth in a glass on the table . . .

CRAWFORD

That's it, Lewbaby, keep it gay . . .

LEWIS

An' it look like she'd been drinkin' this . . . Welch Grape Juice . . . (*a humorless chuckle*) Only she musta spilled it all over her nightgown an' the sheets an' pillowcase. It run down her neck an' got in her hair . . .

CRAWFORD

(*intensely*) Don't stop now, baby, you got a great thing going with the eyes . . .

LEWIS

(*warming to the scene*) So I goes over to the bed, see . . . An' I says to her, I says, hey, Esther, it's way pas' nine. Come on, get up . . . (*with a toneless laugh*) But she don't move none. She just lay there, see, in the bed. With this Welch Grape Juice all over the sheets an' pillow. Only it was dry by then . . . But I couldn't see no empty bottle nor nothin' . . .

CRAWFORD

Yes yes . . .

LEWIS

(*chuckling*) Well, see, I rock her a coupla times, but she's kinda stiff an' don't answer. So I got outa there an' went next door to Mrs. Whitehill. She was the lady lived next door. An' I says to her, come on over, will ya? Looks like somethin' wrong with Esther. She's laying in bed an' won't get up or nothin' . . .

CRAWFORD

(*feverishly*) Go, baby, GO! You got the whole screen!

LEWIS

An' she looks at me, this Mrs. Whitehill, an' says . . . (*giggling*) No, she wouldn't come over cuz she was busy doin' the dishes, see. Whyn't I call a doctor or the cops or somebody like that? She wouldn't help none, see. So what the hell . . . (*He laughs.*) I went an' called this preacher.

CRAWFORD

And Esther?

LEWIS

Why, she just lay there in bed all sopped up with grape juice. She dint get up. Never. Then this preacher come an' says, well, who's gonna look after Lewis now poor Esther's gone?

CRAWFORD

(*exultantly*) Great scene, Lewbaby! Just great!

LEWIS

So he got me this job in the stock room.

CRAWFORD

Absolutely no retakes!

LEWIS

(*shyly pleased*) An' they let me keep that cat. You know that ginger cat me an' Esther had? I kept that cat when I hadda move to that room back a the garage.

CRAWFORD

Yes sir, you even had the lilywhites under control. And the things you had going for you! That little chuckle on the grape juice line. And the eyes! What you had going with the eyes. Boom! Like electricity. I'm still all goose bumps. Look, you gave me gooseflesh on that take. You keep on like this, fella, no telling how long you can last. You read your scenes like this, maybe I won't have to tell after all.

LEWIS

(*alarmed*) Tell? Tell what?

CRAWFORD

No, I said I might not tell.

LEWIS

What's to tell?

CRAWFORD

(*blandly*) Mr. Clark W. Peterson.

LEWIS

(*with growing agitation*) Tell him what? About Esther an' me?

CRAWFORD

No, for God's sake! Use your head, Lewis. You think Peterson gives a damn about you and Esther? What the hell does he care if Esther lay there all sopped up with grape juice?

LEWIS

No, listen, that wasn't really grape juice. I just said that . . .

CRAWFORD

I know it wasn't grape juice, for God's sake! You think I'm some kind of nut or something? Don't be a horse's ass. I'll simply inform Peterson that I been carrying you, that's all. That you don't do a goddam thing back here. I do all the work. And you're just a useless piece of garbage. That's what I'll tell Peterson.

LEWIS

(*frightened*) No, listen, don't say that. He'll can me for sure. Listen, if I promise to help sweep up . . .

CRAWFORD

Get off your knees.

LEWIS

I won't smoke or nothin' . . .

CRAWFORD

Christ Almighty, is that any way to act?

LEWIS

They'll send me up to Camarillo sure as a gun. Please, Crawford, I done nothin' to you.

CRAWFORD

Nothing? I fight like hell to shape you up, and what happens? You go banging on about a haircut you ain't even had. Yakking in my ear about Esther and that preacher and your old cat. You know what happened to that cat of yours? I ate it. I ate that cat. Baked it up in a cat pie and ate it for supper. That's what happened to your cat. (*Crawford frees himself from Lewis's grasp and crosses to the sink, muttering to himself.*) Why waste my time talking to a useless piece of garbage . . .

LEWIS

(*struggling to his feet, frightened*) No, listen, don't say that . . .

CRAWFORD

I'm disappointed in you, Lewis. I don't mind telling you I'm pretty disappointed.

LEWIS

You wouldn't really do that, would ya, Crawford? Tell Peterson? You was only jokin', wasn't ya? Just playin' games on me? Hell, I know you wouldn't do a thing like that. You an' me is buddies. You said so yerself. Ain't that right? Buddies? Hey, I almost fergot. You was gonna tell me that eye story again. You know, how you ripped it out an' . . .

CRAWFORD

(*testily*) Don't you tell it. That's my story.

LEWIS

But you promised.

CRAWFORD

I know what I promised, for God's sake.

LEWIS

(*obsequiously*) You know somethin', I really like that story.

CRAWFORD

You do, huh?

LEWIS

Yeah, that's a real good story.

CRAWFORD

So you wanna hear the Eye Bit.

LEWIS

I sure do, yes sir.

CRAWFORD

You already heard it.

LEWIS

Oh, that don't matter. I always like to hear that story. Honest.

CRAWFORD

Okay, Lewis, for your benefit. The Eye Bit. (*He moves to the center of the room, takes up a stance, and launches into his recitation in staccato fashion without emotion.*) We pan down on this kid. Just six or seven. Just old enough to wipe his nose. There he is on the living room floor. It's a little dark and he's got this knot in his shoelace and can't get it loose. Now cut to this pair of scissors on the table. Big musical sting. Then back to this kid as he reaches out to grab 'em. Cut. Now he's on the floor, stooping over and digging at this knot. He bends down to look close, gets the sharp end into the knot, and gives a real tug. The scissors jerk up and he gets it right in the old eyeball. Get the picture, Lewis? Nice lesson in patience, huh? Now we cut to the school yard. They're yelling at this little kid with the eyepatch. Hey, Cyclops. Hey, dead-eye. Hey, Hathaway. And you know what, Lewis? This kid is laughing. He's really laughing. (*The voice of Peterson is heard on the squawk box.*)

VOICE

Crawford.

CRAWFORD

(*at the box*) Yes sir, Mr. Peterson.

VOICE

Need some help on the checkouts.

CRAWFORD

Coming right out, sir. (*going to the exit, then turning back to Lewis*) What do you want, Lewis? Want me on my knees crying? Think a little thing like that was gonna stop me? Well, you got another think coming, old buddy.

LEWIS

Hey, Crawford, you dint really mean that, did ya . . . ? About eatin' my cat?

CRAWFORD

(*with an enigmatic smile*) What do you think, Lewis? (*He exits.*)

LEWIS

(*calling after him*) Naw, you wouldn't a done nothin' like that. That was my cat. I had that cat from way back. Ever since that cold winter when me an' Esther was livin' over on Lankershim . . . Jeez, it was cold, remember, Crawford? An' we heard this cat outside the house. (*muttering to himself*) He musta got his paws froze out in that cold an' was lost or somethin'. Out there under the porch, hollerin'. So I went out there. Esther come to the door an' says you'll catch yer death. I wasn't wearin' nothin' but my longjohns. An' slippers. Had on a pair a slippers . . . (*Crawford reenters*.) An' there was this little ginger cat out in that cold, with his paws froze up. Why, hell, that cat had ice chunks between his paws big as marbles. I took that cat inside and warmed him real good. Hell, you remember that winter? If I close my eyes real good, I can see that cat lyin' up there on top a the 'frigerator. That was his place, up there over the motor. It was real warm there . . .

CRAWFORD

All right, Lewis, we've heard enough about your cat. Now, just what did you do with my scruples?

LEWIS

(*baffled*) Huh?

CRAWFORD

Come on, come on, what did you do with my scruples?

LEWIS

Wh-a-t?

CRAWFORD

My scru-ples.

LEWIS

What scruples?

CRAWFORD

What scruples? You think I don't have any scruples? Now listen, for your benefit, I had a whole bunch of scruples not more than half an hour ago. Now, what did you do with 'em?

LEWIS

No, listen, I ain't touched 'em. Honest to God.

CRAWFORD

You haven't, huh?

LEWIS

No I ain't.

CRAWFORD

How do you know?

LEWIS

What the hell you mean, how do I know?

CRAWFORD

How do you know you haven't touched 'em?

LEWIS

(*positively*) Because I ain't, that's why!

CRAWFORD

And you're not the kind of man goes around messing with other people's scruples.

LEWIS

No!

CRAWFORD

And you couldn't of touched 'em by accident.

LEWIS

I tell ya I ain't seen 'em, fer crissake!

CRAWFORD

Know what they look like? I bet you wouldn't know a scruple if it was staring you in the face.

LEWIS

(*outraged*) I would too!

CRAWFORD

You would, huh?

LEWIS

Yer damn right I would, sonny!

CRAWFORD

I tell you it's a bad scene when I lose my scruples, Lewis. A real bad scene. Wanna know what happened the first time I lost 'em? Lemme tell you about it. This was a coupla years back. I was working extra at Fox, and one day I saw this guy in the street, see. He had a real great build, nice wavy hair, and two pretty gray eyes, Lewis, with nice long lashes. He was wearing these Levi's with the belt riding low, like this . . . (*showing his belt*) And he had this heavy signet ring on his pinky . . . (*holding up the ring*) I spotted him coming out of Sambo's on Melrose and he got into this Chevy Monza with spoke wheels. So I followed him, Lewis, I followed that guy everywhere he went: Tanny's gym, the laundromat, Von's Market. Then about noon he heads for State

Beach and I'm right after him on my chopper. He parks and goes into that little men's room they got there and strips down to a little pair of white trunks. Then he comes out with his clothes rolled up in a bundle and spreads out his towel and lays back on the sand with two little ginger ale bottle tops over his eyes. Get the picture? Now cut to your old buddy a little ways off, biding his time. And sure enough, pretty soon that guy gets up and trots down for a swim. That was his big mistake, Lewbaby. That was when old Blackjack made his strike.

LEWIS

(*mesmerized*) What'd ya do?

CRAWFORD

Just ambled past where his bundle was lying and when nobody was watching I scooped it up. Pretty soon I was rolling down the Coast Highway with that guy's bundle under my arm. How's that for losing your scruples?

LEWIS

Ahh, I never know what the hell yer talkin' about.

CRAWFORD

It wasn't following that guy that gave me the old thrill, Lewis. It was the identification I felt for him. I wanted to *be* that guy. To get inside his skin. Fit his face over mine. Look out through those pretty gray eyes. And that's just what I did, Lewis. Slipped into his bundle of clothes easy as pie. A couple hours later I headed back up the coast. A cold fog was rolling in. And there he was, wandering up and down the sand, shivering in those swim trunks, wondering what in hell had happened to his clothes. That was one real sad cooky. Don't you see, Lewis? He'd lost his personality. He was nobody. *I* was that guy.

LEWIS

What the hell you mean, you was that guy?

CRAWFORD

That guy is me.

LEWIS

Ahh, you crazy or something? That don't make sense.

CRAWFORD

You think my real name is Crawford? I got names, Lewis. I got a different bundle for every day in the week. (*The voice of Peterson is heard on the squawk box.*)

VOICE

Say, Crawford . . .

CRAWFORD

Yes sir, Mr. Peterson.

VOICE

You got those turnips unloaded?

CRAWFORD

Just finishing up.

VOICE

Pile 'em inside the door and lock up. Let's get the hell out of here. There are still a couple of birds out here. Put 'em back in the box.

CRAWFORD

Check.

VOICE

Oh, say, Crawford . . .

CRAWFORD

Sir?

VOICE

Got something out here for you.

CRAWFORD

Coming right out. (*to Lewis*) Yes siree, Lewis, that was my very first bundle. Still one of my favorites. Be who you want in this life, baby. That's my last word of advice. Change your walk, your talk, anything . . . (*He exits.*)

LEWIS

Be who you want, fer crissake. Change yer walk, yer talk. How the hell can a man do that, I'd like to know . . . (*shouting off*) Just wait'll they get to you, sonny. Wait'll they put you in yer place, that's all I got to say . . . (*muttering sourly*) Change yer life, fer crissake . . . (*Crawford appears in the doorway carrying a small, table-size Christmas tree, fully decorated.*)

CRAWFORD

Look here, Lewis. See what Mr. Clark W. Peterson has presented the boys in the back room.

LEWIS

(*awed*) That thing ours?

CRAWFORD

Pretty generous, wouldn't you say? Lewbaby, shall we put her up?

LEWIS

Has it got lights?

CRAWFORD

Has it got lights. This tree was out in Meats and Poultry, Lewis. You think they'd allow a tree in Meats and Poultry without lights?

LEWIS

(*eagerly*) Can we plug her in?

CRAWFORD

Why not?

LEWIS

Peterson won't care?

CRAWFORD

Peterson's gone home. It's after closing and all the little Petersons are waiting to pass go and collect their two hundred. Nobody left but us, old buddy. You and me and ten sacks of turnips. So why not have our own little celebration? (*He hunts for a plug outlet.*)

LEWIS

I dint have no tree last year. We always had a tree back home. Every year.

CRAWFORD

(*plugging in the cord*) Now, Lewis . . . There!

LEWIS

(*softly*) Say, now . . .

CRAWFORD

How about that? Does that take you back, Lewbaby?

LEWIS

Jesus . . . that sure is pretty . . .

CRAWFORD

> (*intoning*) Our Father which art in heaven, Give us this day our Christmas tree . . . You didn't know I was religious, did you, Lewis? Hell yes, I was born religious . . . (*He begins stacking sacks of turnips near the rear door.*)

LEWIS

> When I was a kid, we always went over to the church there on Woodland . . . (*gazing at the tree, speaking more softly*) Every Christmas . . . Glen Avon Church right there on Woodland . . .

CRAWFORD

> (*as he stacks turnips at the rear*) Know what my old lady told me, Lewis? At the very hour of my birth, this little statue of the Virgin burst into tears. This little BVM which glowed in the dark at the side of her bed burst into tears . . . No kidding.

LEWIS

> We used to sit by the tree . . . I can remember that. Singin' songs. And they had this candy handout. You know, popcorn strung on a thread an' cookies an' hot cider. I remember that . . .

CRAWFORD

> (*coming from the rear*) You didn't know my old lady was a saint, did you, Lewis? Oh yes, that woman had a direct line straight through to Jesus on the royal telephone.

LEWIS

> (*beginning to sing in a faltering, hoarse voice as he squats looking at the tree*) "Silent night, holy night . . ."

CRAWFORD

> That woman was holy, all right. So holy the dishes were four days in the sink while she was busy with her church circle. (*He goes toward the rear.*) I'm locking up, Lewis. Turnips are all tucked in bed . . .

LEWIS

> "All is calm, all is bright . . ."

CRAWFORD

> (*from the rear*) And in consequence of her great love, Our Lord did anything he could for her. Sent her every kind of trial there was. Finally stretched her out on a bed of pain . . .

LEWIS

(*singing very low*) "Silent night . . ."

CRAWFORD

(*coming forward, gazing at Lewis*) Why, that's like a picture, Lewis. All we need is a little organ music in the background . . . Yes sir, her body was wasted. Eaten. But no complaints. No complaints. I remember those long, sad afternoons. I knew something was wrong with her. I could see the pain in her eyes and this twisted smile pasted to her face. But she'd only say, oh, I'm all right, sonny. God is looking after me. His eye is on the sparrow. Once I saw her feeling this thing in her stomach. This big lump. Hard, like a cake of soap under the skin. Why don't you go to the doctor? I said. Oh, I'll be all right. Never you mind about me. But she'd get out of bed to go to church. Oh yes, she never missed her church. Standing there at the back door, trying to put on her gloves, her mouth all twisted up, the knuckles white where she grabbed the table to hold on. Oh, I tell you, Lewis, she had a chance to get in there and really suffer for the Lord. (*He stands behind Lewis, resting his hands on his shoulders.*) Don't stop. I like that singing, I really do.

LEWIS

I'm cold . . .

CRAWFORD

(*putting a gunnysack around his shoulders*) That better? (*Lewis nods.*) Toward the end when the cancer was really at her, the heat of her body was so hot you couldn't touch her. She died weighing ninety-two pounds. That saintly woman had wasted away to ninety-two pounds. And then you know what happened, Lewis? After she died? The doctors made this autopsy, and you know what they found embedded in her liver? This little snapshot of Jesus. Tiny snapshot of Jesus in sepia, right there in her liver. And he was grinning, Lewis. How about that . . .

LEWIS

We used to sing like that every Christmas back home, sittin' by the tree . . . (*Crawford moves to the locker and takes a gaily wrapped cylinder from it. He returns to Lewis.*) What's that?

CRAWFORD

It's Christmas, isn't it? Now, you didn't think Blackjack would forget his buddy, did you?

LEWIS

(*shyly*) Fer me?

CRAWFORD

(*handing him the package*) Isn't much, baby. Wish it could be more.

LEWIS

(*taking it gingerly*) Aww, you shouldn't a done that.

CRAWFORD

Open it.

LEWIS

But I ain't got nothin' fer you.

CRAWFORD

The thought for the deed, Lewis. The thought for the deed.

LEWIS

(*opening the package*) What is this anyway? (*He rips off the wrapping paper and holds up a calendar faced with a large colored photo of a cat.*)

CRAWFORD

That's a calendar, Lewis.

LEWIS

Calendar?

CRAWFORD

And see, you got a different cat for every month. You got twelve cats there. Look at those pictures. Pretty, huh?

LEWIS

Well, say, that sure is nice . . . I sure do appreciate having this thing . . .

CRAWFORD

That's your cat calendar, Lewis. That's Lewis Sopko's private cat calendar for the new year. Now whenever you wanna check the date, you just glance up to the wall and there it is, with this big cat grinning down in full color.

LEWIS

Well, say . . .

CRAWFORD

I just hope it'll remind you of old Crawford after he's gone.

LEWIS

Gone?

CRAWFORD

Didn't I tell you?

LEWIS

Tell me what?

CRAWFORD

You mean I forgot to tell my old buddy?

LEWIS

(*alarmed*) Tell what, fer crissake?

CRAWFORD

That Blackjack's moving on?

LEWIS

On? You mean yer goin' somewhere?

CRAWFORD

(*quietly*) That's right, Lewbaby. I'm finished with this stock boy routine as of today. Gonna strike this warehouse set, pack my props, and move on.

LEWIS

(*growing more alarmed*) You ain't leavin'?!

CRAWFORD

It's in the cards, baby.

LEWIS

But you can't! (*Crawford goes to the footlocker and begins to remove his personal effects, putting them in a flight bag.*)

CRAWFORD

You think I was gonna spend the rest of my life in this dump? Listen, I got plans. The time'll come when you'll read about old Blackjack in the papers, see me on the ten o'clock news. Glare of the kliegs, sirens screaming, big black Caddies, flashbulbs popping. And when I come on, Lewis, the cops'll lose control. Thousands will stampede and scream in the crush, just to get one look, just to touch . . . (*He exits into the store.*)

LEWIS

(*calling after him in anguish*) But what about me? What's gonna happen to me, Crawford? I got rights! (*hoarsely*) Who's gonna do yer work? Who they gonna put in here? How do I know I'll get along with him . . . ? (*turning back*) That's a helluva thing, sneakin' off like that. I shoulda known that young punk would pull a stunt like that . . . duckin' out on me . . . (*thinking desperately*) How do I know they ain't gonna send me up to Camarillo? (*with sudden decision*) I got to get down to Lynwood. Get hold a that preacher. They'll do that sure as a gun, send me up to Camarillo . . . (*Lewis stumbles toward the sink, upsetting Crawford's bundle of personal effects onto the dirty floor. He snatches Crawford's towel and soap and begins feverishly washing his hands. Crawford enters from the store carrying two limp turkeys by the neck. He puts down the birds and crosses to Lewis and viciously rips the towel from his hands. Lewis whirls in confusion and terror.*)

CRAWFORD

Just what the hell you think you're doing? Gimme that thing. Christ Almighty! You think I want your germs crawling over my towel?! (*picking up his personal belongings*) Look at my things! Just what the hell are you up to anyhow?

LEWIS

(*cringing*) Just washin' up. Gonna get down to Lynwood, see that preacher . . .

CRAWFORD

(*ominously*) You went too far, buddy. This time you really went too far.

LEWIS

Huh?

CRAWFORD
>Screwing around with my things.

LEWIS
>Dint mean it, honest to God, Crawford . . .

CRAWFORD
>Look at that towel. Now I got to burn it.

LEWIS
>No no, it only needs washin', that's all . . .

CRAWFORD
>You know the rules back here. How many times do I have to tell you? You think I want some crummy disease?

LEWIS
>I got no disease . . .

CRAWFORD
>You're sick.

LEWIS
>No, listen, Crawford, I ain't sick . . .

CRAWFORD
>I say you're sick.

LEWIS
>Doctors gimme a clean bill, when I come here, company doc gimme a clean bill.

CRAWFORD
>Did you say clean? Look at that towel. Clean! You don't know the meaning of the word. (*with sudden decision, snatching up a doctor's green smock from his personal effects and putting it on*) If you had such a clean bill, maybe you won't mind if I run a few tests of my own . . . If you got such a clean bill we'll soon find out . . .

LEWIS
>(*fearfully*) Where'd you get that thing?

CRAWFORD
>(*blandly*) Didn't you see the call sheet, Lewis? Doctor's Examination Scene, that's what it says.

LEWIS

Since when are you a doctor?

CRAWFORD

Oh, I've read a few things. I figure I could give you a little going over. (*adjusting an eye-reflector to his head*) Bet you'd like to know how old Blackjack picked up this particular bundle, wouldn't you? (*taking out his pad and pencil*) Shall we get started?

LEWIS

I don't wanna play . . .

CRAWFORD

(*businesslike, official*) Name?

LEWIS

Whacha mean, name?

CRAWFORD

Your name?

LEWIS

You already know my name, fer crissake.

CRAWFORD

(*patiently*) Look, Lewis, you wanna play the scene, you gotta follow the script. Now, what's your name?

LEWIS

Lewis.

CRAWFORD

You got a last name, Lewis?

LEWIS

(*timidly*) Sopko.

CRAWFORD

Would you kindly speak up.

LEWIS

Sopko.

CRAWFORD

What kind of name is that? Lewis Sopko. Listen to the sound of that name. Lewisss Sop-ko . . . That name lacks pedigree. Another twenty years, a man won't be allowed to go around with a shabby name like that. Another twenty years, people will have pedigree too, just like dogs. That isn't too much to ask, is it? With the world getting more crowded by the minute? These humanitarians who go around curing disease, giving people medicine and charity, that's all fuzzy thinking. That only keeps the misfits in the game. We don't need more hospitals. What we need is more morgues. Occupation?

LEWIS

    I ain't no misfit. You callin' me a misfit?

CRAWFORD

    (*patiently*) Your occupation.

LEWIS

    Listen here, I ain't on relief! I got a job.

CRAWFORD

    Just what is this job of yours?

LEWIS

    (*defiantly*) I sweep up.

CRAWFORD

    (*writing on the pad*) Occupation: sweeps up. Where?

LEWIS

    Right here, right back a the market. I sweep up.

CRAWFORD

    All right, Mr. Sopko. Any birth injuries? Clubfoot? Lung trouble? No umbilical cord round your neck choking you? What's that popeyed look supposed to mean? Afraid you're not giving the doctor much cooperation, Mr. Sopko. Any fear of the dark? Nightmares? Thumb-sucking? You bite your nails? (*swiftly taking his hand*) Lemme see those nails? Ahh ha! You any idea how revealing this is? (*Lewis jerks his hand away.*) Any history of enuresis? You piddle at night? How about stuttering? Say "cat." "Cat."

LEWIS

    Why should I?

CRAWFORD

    Just say "cat."

LEWIS

Say, what is this anyhow!

CRAWFORD

Strictly clinical, Mr. Sopko. Chronic use of drugs? Family history of epilepsy? Alcoholism? Please try to concentrate. These questions are highly relevant.

LEWIS

Doctor already gimme a clean bill . . .

CRAWFORD

Now, would you say you were the shy type? Reserved? You do a lot of daydreaming? Suspicious of people? Harbor any ill will toward anybody, any group or sect?

LEWIS

Why should I?

CRAWFORD

No excessive hatred of wino barbers, for instance?

LEWIS

Say, what is this? What you writin' down there?

CRAWFORD

Are you a neat person?

LEWIS

Yer damn right.

CRAWFORD

You'd characterize yourself as aggressively neat and orderly?

LEWIS

Damn right I would.

CRAWFORD

(*writing*) "Aggressively neat and orderly." Now repeat after me: Eight - four - seven - nine - five - three. Eight - seven - four - five - nine - three. You seem confused, Mr. Sopko. Are you confused?

LEWIS

(*whirling around*) I'm gettin' outa here! (*He rushes wildly toward the door. Crawford follows, firing questions at him.*)

CRAWFORD

No recent attempts at self-injury? No hallucinations? No cat tracks in the pancake batter? Speak up, speak up! (*He suddenly takes up a flashlight and flashes it in Lewis's eyes.*) Does this bother you?

LEWIS

Get that outa my eyes!

CRAWFORD

What does the early bird catch? Does a potato hurt when peeled? Does cloth scream when torn?

LEWIS

(*trying to thrash away from him*) What the hell . . .

CRAWFORD

(*pursuing*) Does cloth scream when torn?

LEWIS

How should I know?

CRAWFORD

Well, listen! (*With sudden savagery, Crawford rips the shirt off Lewis's back, at the same time shrieking in a high-pitched voice. Lewis stares dumbly, immobilized with fear. Crawford speaks quietly.*) You hear a scream?

LEWIS

(*huddling in his sleeveless gray underwear*) Look what you done. You tore my shirt.

CRAWFORD

Did you hear a scream?

LEWIS

Yes . . .

CRAWFORD

What was it like? Describe what you heard.

LEWIS

Just a scream. Like someone was hurt . . .

CRAWFORD

You're sure about that? (*Lewis nods dumbly. Crawford writes on the note pad.*) "Patient suffers marked degree of auditory hallucination." (*smiling at Lewis*) I believe you hear things, Mr. Sopko.

LEWIS

> I dint hear nothin'.

CRAWFORD

> You didn't hear that shirt scream?

LEWIS

> It was you screamed.

CRAWFORD

> But you said just now that shirt screamed.

LEWIS

> Listen, Crawford, we played long enough.

CRAWFORD

> This is no game, Lewis. We're not playing now.

LEWIS

> Please, Crawford . . .

CRAWFORD

> I seem to recall the first thing you said this morning, something about hearing a cat. (*He meows like a cat.*) You remember that cat, Lewis? No, this is pretty serious if you ask me. You hear things.

LEWIS

> I gotta go now. It's way pas' six . . .

CRAWFORD

> You don't wanna hear the results of your exam? (*He taps the note pad.*) It's all here. Progressive psychosis. Hallucinations, loss of coherence, disordered memory, irritability . . .

LEWIS

> (*dumbly*) Doctors already gimme a clean bill.

CRAWFORD

> Kindly remove your pants.

LEWIS

> Wha-a-t?

CRAWFORD

> Kindly take off your pants. (*Lewis stares at him.*) Didn't you see the call sheet? It was on the call plain as day. "Doctor's Examination Scene." Lewis Sopko in socks and underwear. Don't look

scared, Lewis. Nothing to be scared of. You play a doctor's examination scene, naturally you expect to remove your pants. Now kindly take 'em off.

LEWIS

(*piteously*) If I do, will ya lemme go then? I really gotta get down to Lynwood.

CRAWFORD

This won't take a minute, Mr. Sopko. (*Cowed and frightened, Lewis slowly removes his trousers and drops them near his ripped shirt.*) Well, thank you. Now maybe we can get on with the scene. (*He gathers Lewis's clothes into a bundle.*) Three times through the Bendix with Lysol and a fluff-dry, that's what I recommend for this bundle, Lewis. (*throwing the clothes down*) Now the shoes . . . Shoes, please . . . (*Lewis stares at him, then hesitantly removes his shoes. Crawford looks gravely at the pitiful Lewis standing before him in his socks and gray underwear, then slowly shakes his head.*) Who fitted you with this costume? Were you up at wardrobe? Did somebody send you up to wardrobe? (*calling off stage*) Where's the wardrobe mistress! Who's responsible for this? (*to Lewis*) You know better than to come on the set in a rig like this! What's this lingerie you got on? This what the senior citizen is wearing this year?

LEWIS

(*miserably*) Please, Crawford, I'm cold . . .

CRAWFORD

Not even any makeup? What's the trouble? Couldn't you find your skin tone on the cosmetic chart? (*rubbing a finger over Lewis's forehead*) Not even a foundation cream. No angelshade makeup base. Seems to me you came unprepared, Lewbaby. I don't believe you primped one little bit for the final scene, did you? Just came as you are. Well, that's a big mistake, buddy. There comes a time when a man can't afford to make any more mistakes.

LEWIS

> (*whining piteously*) Gimme my clothes now, Crawford. I really gotta go. It's way pas' six . . .

CRAWFORD

> Now you know the secret, don't you, buddy? Now you get the message. Stay young, stay with it. Hair and walk and spit, all young and elastic. That's the big secret. As long as your skin is clear you got it made. Doesn't matter what you do, who you screw, how you operate. Just stay with it. That's war, buddy. That's the real race war. Between young and old. You and me. I'm still in there, but you, old buddy. I tried like hell. I worked like a dog to check you out. Gave you every test there was to shape you up. But I'm afraid you just don't make the grade any more. And I'm sorry about that. I really am . . . (*Crawford looks sadly at Lewis, then abruptly crosses to his locker and removes his doctor's gown and eye-reflector. Lewis watches him for a long moment.*)

LEWIS

> (*at last*) We . . . done playin' now?

CRAWFORD

> (*stuffing clothes into the flight bag*) That's right, baby. (*nodding toward the turkeys on the table*) Gotta get our birds back in the box and lock up.

LEWIS

> (*visibly relieved*) You know what? You really had me scared back there. I thought you was really gonna let 'em send me up to Camarillo.

CRAWFORD

> Just another game, Lewbaby. Just another game. (*Smiling sadly, Crawford crosses to Lewis.*) But all kidding aside, Lewis. It's late. The scene is over. I'm sorry as hell, baby, but that's the way it is. You gotta be ruthless in this world. I'm a reasonable man, I'm willing to be shown. But I'm afraid you just don't make the grade. The laughs aren't there any more. I love my Lewis, I really do. My heart bleeds for you, but I gotta be strong.

LEWIS

You mean you really ain't comin' back? Ain't gonna be here Monday mornin'? (*Crawford gazes mutely at Lewis, shakes his head, rises abruptly, and exits into the store to lock up. Lewis follows him to the door; he speaks in an anguished voice.*) No, Crawford, listen to me . . . We had good times, dint we? We had a lotta good times back here, dint we . . . ? Crawford . . . (*Crawford reenters and begins turning out the lights. Lewis follows him, babbling on.*) We was always buddies, you and me. Ain't that right? Buddies? Hey, you wanna hear that about Esther again? You always liked that story. Want me to tell you about Esther and the grape juice again?

CRAWFORD

(*gently*) We already had the Esther Bit today, Lewbaby.

LEWIS

(*wildly*) Well, listen . . . Hey, I know! I never told you about my cat, how that cat quit on me, did I? You wanna hear about that?

CRAWFORD

Is it pretty funny?

LEWIS

Hell yes it's funny!

CRAWFORD

Well, make it fast. And remember, keep it light and gay. Lots of laughs.

LEWIS

Well, see . . . Lemme tell ya about this. One night I dint come home and feed him like I always done, see. I stayed out all night drinkin' beer. So when I finally come home, musta been around five or six, I sneaked in that little room where I was stayin' back a the garage. I dint wanna wake that cat, see . . . What the hell you doin'?

CRAWFORD

(*lighting a single candle and placing it upright on a box*) Just setting up. Little dab of cotton. Holy oil. The old mumbo-jumbo.

LEWIS

(*angrily*) Listen to this!

CRAWFORD

(*quietly*) I hear you, Lewis.

LEWIS

No, see, he wasn't there. That cat wasn't there. He always slept curled up at the foot a my bed, but that cat was gone . . . (*chuckling remorselessly*) That was his way of gettin' even fer my bein' out all night. He drew the line at that, see . . . Hell, that cat knew! Don't tell me that cat dint know! I looked fer that cat.

CRAWFORD

Did you, Lewis? (*He takes a small piece of cotton and makes motions in the air before Lewis's face.*)

LEWIS

(*vehemently*) Hell yes I looked! Trampin' up and down the woods back there, in the tall grass . . . I looked fer that cat. But he'd gone. He never come back, Crawford . . . (*He attempts to laugh, begins to break down.*) That cat never come back.

CRAWFORD

That's too bad, Lewis, I'm really sorry to hear that.

LEWIS

(*breaking completely, sinking to his knees*) Just wait'll you got nothin' left but an old alley cat. Wait'll that's all you got left . . . (*weeping bitterly, beating the cement floor with his fists*) Goddam that cat, leavin' me like that. Goddam him anyway . . .

CRAWFORD

(*gazing down with compassion as Lewis weeps helplessly*) You're right, Lewbaby, that's a pretty funny story at that. (*He makes the sign of the cross over him, intoning.*) In Nomine Patris, Filius, et Spiritus Sanctus . . . (*He bends to raise Lewis up.*) Now come on, baby. It's late.

LEWIS

(*sobbing*) That cat was just punishin' me, Crawford. I dint feed him that night . . .

CRAWFORD

That's right, you forgot to feed him and he was punishing you. Now come on, time to close up for the night. (*pointing to the turkeys on the table*) You put those birds back in the box. Will you do that little favor for Mr. Clark W. Peterson?

LEWIS

(*dumbly taking the birds*) That cat's gone fer good, Crawford. Ain't never comin' back . . .

CRAWFORD

(*as Lewis moves toward the coldbox door*) Afriad not, baby. Now you tuck those birds in bed like a good lad . . . (*Lewis disappears into the coldbox. Crawford looks after him for a moment, then crosses silently to the heavy double door and slides the bolt into place. He returns to the sink and begins meticulously washing his hands. A dull pounding is heard from inside the coldbox. Crawford turns off the water and looks around for something on which to dry his hands; finally he takes up the bundle of Lewis's clothes and carefully wipes each finger dry. The pounding continues from inside the coldbox together with the muffled sounds of Lewis calling out. Crawford picks up his flight bag and, whistling softly to himself, goes to the door at the rear. Then he turns, crosses back into the room, and snuffs out the candle. The stock room is now dark save for the tiny lights glowing on the Christmas tree. Crawford returns to the exit and goes out, locking the door after him. The dull pounding continues to echo in the silence of the empty stock room as the lights on the Christmas tree dim slowly down and out.*)

Production History

Do Not Pass Go was first produced at the Cherry Lane Theater in New York in 1965. The play was subsequently produced at the Theatre-in-the-Round in Minneapolis (1966), at the Margo Jones Theater in Dallas (1968), and at a number of European theaters.

Original Cast

Crawford .... Charles M. Nolte

Lewis................................. Roberts Blossom

Directed by Alan Schneider

Do Not Pass Go at the Cherry Lane Theater in New York in April 1965.
Actor Roberts Blossom as Lewis and actor/playwright Charles Nolte as
Crawford. (Photographs by Miss Alix Jeffry.)

Georg Büchner's **Woyzeck**

Adapted by David Ball

Comments

This script is an acting adaptation of *Woyzeck,* not a close translation of the German original. It was written with the immediate purpose of putting the play on stage. I have tried to accent those portions of the incomplete fragments that I find theatrically valuable, and I have altered or ignored those portions that do not seem to me to work. Where I have changed, added, or deleted, I can defend the work only pragmatically. I have not tried to "finish" Büchner's uncompleted script because it is that sense of incompleteness that gives the play much of its power. I have simply rendered this collection of fragments as coherent and playable as possible.

A word about the order of the scenes. It is possible to produce this play successfully with its scenes in almost any order. I have chosen one way — and it is only one of several — to build the intensity of the play without forcing a rhythm, but little would be obscured or wrenched if another order were chosen. Internal evidence regarding Büchner's intention is ambiguous at best, and external evidence, where it exists, is incomplete enough to be useless. Again, my approach was pragmatic: I chose the order I thought would be most effective, and can think of no better defense.

This harrowing play, decently produced, will reach any audience at any time. It is one of those plays that cannot be "interpreted"; it is simply a raw, jagged story of what happened to a man, of what a man did. The play has become one of the archetypes of modern drama, a great influence on almost every major dramatist of the past seventy-five years. It belonged to no established tradition when it was written in 1836, and even today it can be classified only with those plays that have heavily imitated it. It has been called expressionist, naturalistic, tragic, absurd, a social play, a psychological play, a theological play, an intimate play, and a cosmic play. Somehow a twenty-three-year-old playwright managed to write a play that fits all of these descriptions. His early death may have cost us one of the half-dozen giants of theater. There is certainly no play comparable to *Woyzeck* by so young a playwright. And certainly no other single play has so influenced the course of twentieth-century drama.

David Ball

Woyzeck

Characters

Woyzeck
Captain
Andre
Marie
Idiot
Margret
Drum Major
Old Man
Charlatan
Sergeant
Proprietor
Doctor
First Apprentice
Second Apprentice
Jew
Girl
Grandmother
Kathy
Police Chief
Musicians
Townspeople

Scene i

At the Captain's.

CAPTAIN

Woyzeck, slow down! Slow down! I'm getting dizzy. If you're done early, I'll be stuck with six extra minutes. What am I supposed to do with six excess minutes? Think, Woyzeck, give this a thought: you've got thirty years to go, thirty endless years to live. Thirty! You know how long that is? Three hundred and sixty months. Not to mention days. And the hours, the minutes! All packed into thirty years. What will you do with that ghastly stretch of time? Do you ever think about things like that, Woyzeck?

WOYZECK

Yes sir, Captain.

CAPTAIN

My brain breaks down when I think about the world. The world, Woyzeck. Think of it! And eternity! Eternity and the world! Humankind's function, Woyzeck: the function of man, that's the eternal, that's the infinite. Eternity gapes at us every day. Can you understand that? Every day, Woyzeck. Infinite, eternal man . . . but on the other hand, a mere drop in time's bucket. Splash and it's over, leaving naught but ripples receding into the eternal. A grain of sand in the hand of the ocean. A moment. No more.

Woyzeck, my brain reels when I consider that the earth turns itself all the way around every single day. What a waste of time. And what for? Where will it lead? Around and around. Woyzeck, it saddens me to watch a waterwheel.

WOYZECK

Yes sir, Captain.

CAPTAIN

Cheer up, Woyzeck. It's not all that bad. Nothing is. You think too much. Good men don't think and get depressed. Good men with good consciences, that is. So? Say something, Woyzeck. Talk, will you? What's the weather today?

WOYZECK

Bad, Captain sir. Wind.

CAPTAIN

Wind, yes. I can feel it here, Woyzeck, deep inside. I feel the wind in my gut. It's bad out there. I'm affected the same way by spiders. (*slyly*) That wind must be out of the north-south.

WOYZECK

Yes sir, Captain.

CAPTAIN

Ha! Haha! Numbskull! North-south. You are exquisitely stupid. You must be a happy man. (*moved*) And you're a good man, Woyzeck, a good person. But (*with dignity*) you have no morals, Woyzeck — you have a child without the blessing of the church. That's what our right reverend platoon chaplain says: "Without the blessing of the church." It isn't *my* phrase.

WOYZECK

Captain sir, the good Lord's not going to be hard on a poor child just because I didn't say "Amen" before I went at it. The Lord says, "Suffer little children to come unto me."

CAPTAIN

What? What? What are you talking about? You're crazy, Woyzeck, you talked all those words without saying a thing. You're confusing me, Woyzeck. I AM YOUR CAPTAIN! Explain.

WOYZECK

Captain sir, with us poor people, it's — if you — money, sir! Money. Without money you — well — morals. How can anyone have morals when he's bringing someone like me into the world? I'm just flesh and blood, Captain, that's all. I'm — if I ever get into heaven they'll make me help with the thunder.

CAPTAIN

Woyzeck, you lack virtue. You are not a virtuous human being. Flesh and blood? I look out my window, my eyes following those stockinged legs slithering by — damn, Woyzeck! I feel love too, you know, I know all about flesh and blood. But virtue, Woyzeck! Dignity! I find other ways to use my time. I say to myself, as I let those stockings disappear around the corner, I say to myself (*moved*), "You're a virtuous man, a decent, good man."

WOYZECK

Yes, Captain sir, virtue. I don't have much. But us ordinary people — we — what happens to us, it's nature. Not virtue. That's how it is. But if I was a gentleman, if I had a hat and a watch and a cane, if I talked smooth like you — then I'd have virtue, all right. I'll bet there's something good about having virtue. But I'm just ordinary, Captain. Good for nothing.

CAPTAIN

But good nevertheless, Woyzeck. Only you think too much. It eats you up, it wears you down. Stop thinking bad things. Stop thinking altogether. Woyzeck, this discussion has moved me. You may leave now. But don't run! Slow down! Slow down, Woyzeck!

Scene ii

In a field.

WOYZECK

There's a curse on this place, Andre. See where the grass is faded? Toadstools, Andre. Heads roll through here at night. Someone picked one up, once. He thought it was a hedgehog. Three days, three nights, he was in a wood box. (*low*) Andre! I understand it. It was the Freethinkers.

ANDRE

(*singing**)

    Two rabbits sat in the deepest grass
    Gnawing along the green green lawn . . .

WOYZECK

Shhh! Andre! Listen! Something's moving.

ANDRE

(*singing*)

    Gnawing along the green green lawn
    Till the lawn was gone from the ground.

WOYZECK

It's behind us. Underneath. (*stamping*) It's hollow. Listen. The Freethinkers, Andre. Moving.

ANDRE

Let's go.

WOYZECK

Strange how it's quiet. Shh. Hold your breath, Andre. Listen! (*pause*) Andre!

ANDRE

What?

WOYZECK

(*to the ground*) Say something! (*He looks around.*) Andre! Look.

*Music on page 134.

The whole sky's on fire, and there's a noise coming down like trumpets. It's getting closer. Come on. Don't look at it. (*He drags Andre into the bushes.*)

ANDRE

(*after a pause*) Do you still hear it?

WOYZECK

No. It's gone. Quiet. Like the world's dead. (*Drums are heard in the distance.*)

ANDRE

We've got to go. Come on.

Scene iii

At Marie's. Outside the soldiers march with the sound of drums. The Drum Major goes by. The Idiot enters with Marie's baby.

IDIOT

(*rocking the child*) Rat-a-tat-tat! Rat-a-tat-tat! (*He gives the child to Marie.*)

MARIE

Ho, boy! Rat-a-tat-tat. Rat-a-tat-tat. Hear them? There they are.

MARGRET

(*as the Drum Major passes*) Look at that man! Built like a tree!

MARIE

He moves like a knife! (*The Drum Major salutes Marie.*)

MARGRET

Did you see that look, neighbor? And you looked back. We're not used to that kind of thing from you, Marie.

MARIE

(*singing*)
Soldiers, oh you shining lads . . .

MARGRET

Your eyes are shining.

MARIE

So? What's it to you? Shine *your* eyes and take them to the pawnshop. Maybe the old Jew will buy them for buttons.

MARGRET

Listen to her! Look here, Virgin Mary, who do you think you're talking to? I've got some decency in me — but everyone's seen you stare your way through seven layers of leather pants.

MARIE

Bitch. (*She moves away with the child; Margret leaves.*) Come on, Christian. What's the difference? Even if your ma's a whore, your little bastard face still makes her happy. (*She sings a wordless lullaby.* It is interrupted by a knock at the window.*) Franz? Is that you? (*Woyzeck enters.*)

WOYZECK

I can't stay. There's roll call.

MARIE

Did you cut the Captain's wood?

WOYZECK

Yes, Marie.

MARIE

Franz — what's the matter? (*During the following speeches the Idiot, now outside, quietly sings the lullaby tune.*)

WOYZECK

It happened again. Only more. Doesn't the Bible say, "And there arose a smoke from under the ground, as the smoke of great furnaces"?

MARIE

Franz, you—

WOYZECK

Shh. I understand it. The Freethinkers — they're down under there. And there was noise in the sky and fire. I'm finding something out, I'm finding it out and it followed me all the way

*Music on page 134.

back. It followed me — but I can't get my hands on it. It won't show when I look straight at it. It drives people mad. What's it there for?

MARIE

Franz—

WOYZECK

Can't you see? Look around. Look, everything sharp and hard, nothing moving, everything gray. Back there — something's moving . . . When God goes, everything follows. I'll see you tonight — at the fair. I've saved something. (*Woyzeck leaves; the Idiot stops singing.*)

MARIE

It's gloomy in here. Christian! Why so quiet? Scared? Look how dark it's getting. Like our eyes were going out. (*She starts singing the lullaby again. Outside, the Idiot curls up and sleeps. Marie stops singing abruptly.*) Let's get out of here. The walls are staring.

Scene iv

At the fair.

OLD MAN

(*singing**)
     Nothing on this earth can last,
     Life is like the summer grass;
     The world's too fast, too fast, too fast . . .

WOYZECK

Ah! Poor old man. You were young once. Like me. Fun and sorrow, trouble and fun . . .

*Music on page 134.

MARIE

When fools make sense, we're all fools. The world is crazy! Hold my arm, Franz.

CHARLATAN

Gentlemen! Gentlemen! Ladies! Gather around, look into this hole before you. The pit, ladies and gentlemen, the black pit. But look closely — what do you see?

MARIE

(to Woyzeck) Franz! He's got a monkey in there!

CHARLATAN

A creature as God made him — a beast, an animal, stinking right here before your eyes. But look! I shine this light on him; he looks up at me, squinting, blinded — his filthy pit brightens — and he walks, ladies and gentlemen, he stands upright and walks (ooohs and ahhs from the crowd) . . . prances, struts. Look at him jump and come down on two feet. And see his coat? A perfect soldier! Even carries a saber! He's not much different, ladies and gentlemen; in fact he's exactly the same. He lives in a dirt hole: he's a soldier. When I turn out the light, he lies down. And my friends, just step inside and you'll find the galactic horse and every kind of *freakus homo sapientosis*. The horse; the horse; you must see the horse. Just step right in. You can find out anything you want — your age, how many children you have, will have, used to have — what your sorrows are. Why you are sick, how to get well. The show is about to start. And it starts, ladies and gentlemen, at the beginning — the very beginning. The little creature in the hole was just an introduction. Aren't you? (*He looks into the hole.*) Hey! He got away! (*He runs off after the monkey.*)

WOYZECK

I once had this dog who licked my feet when I snapped my fingers.

A GENTLEMAN

That's disgusting.

WOYZECK

Sir, it's an honest fact that I don't believe in God — don't you either? Why is that disgusting? I like things that *are* disgusting.

See there? A man climbing a tree after a monkey. That disgusting
enough for you? (*to Marie*) Want to go in?

MARIE
Come on! The man inside's got tassels on his hat. And his wife's
got pants on. (*They go in.*)

DRUM MAJOR
You see that one?

SERGEANT
Built for breeding regiments.

DRUM MAJOR
And drum majors!

SERGEANT
Look how she holds that head. Like all that black hair could drag
her down like a weight. Did you see her eyes?

DRUM MAJOR
Like staring down a well. Come on . . .

Scene v

Inside a bright booth.

MARIE
Look at these lights.

WOYZECK
Like burning eyes on black cats. What a night, Marie. What a
night.

PROPRIETOR
Ladies and gentlemen, gather round. Cast your eyes into this stall.
My friends, the horse you see installed here, standing on four legs,
a tail on its torso, has one of the finest minds in Europe — not
only for a horse, but for learned professors as well. (*to the horse*)

Put human society to shame! Show your animal reasoning. Ladies and gentlemen, when this animal isn't here, he's off at the university where he's a professor of history and dean of men. Of course that's not much of an achievement; it requires only simple intelligence. But (*to the horse*) show your complex intelligence. Stamp your hoof three times.

PROPRIETOR'S WIFE

One! Two! Three!

PROPRIETOR

Ah! There. Now. I will ask a question of more delicacy: is there a jackass in this learned assembly? (*pause*) You see, gentlemen and ladies? Not only can he reason to answer the question, but he knows enough to be polite and keep the answer to himself. This is physiognomy in action, friends! This is no brute; this is a human being in a stall. A person! Yet still an animal, a beast of nature. Just look down, look at the floor of his stall — see, he has put human society to shame. And he is still, as you can see, in a state of nature himself. Not ideal nature, but nature is nature. Learn from this, ladies and gentlemen. You will be better ladies and gentlemen for it. And what can we learn from this, you might ask? Ah! Well might you ask, and if this horse deigned to talk instead of neigh, he would tell you: "You are created of dirt, dust, and dung." And who says we must be more than dirt, dust, and dung? Some of us are more dirt than dust, some more dust than dung, some more dung than dirt and dust, but it all comes down to the same thing. So this horse would tell you, and he can count to three — but he cannot express himself, can't explain. A transformed human being! (*to the horse*) Tell the people what time it is. Who has a watch? Someone give me their watch.

SERGEANT

(*holding out a watch to the horse*) A watch, my good sir.

MARIE

I've got to see this! (*She shoves her way through the crowd. The Sergeant steps aside for her. She stands near the stall next to the Drum Major. He looks at her. She stares back.*)

Scene vi

In Marie's room. Marie sits with the child. The Idiot is in a corner on the floor. Marie looks at her earrings in a piece of broken mirror. She talks to herself and to the child, never to the Idiot.

MARIE

He ordered Franz to go; what could I do? (*She looks at herself.*) Look at the stones shine. I wonder if they're real? Maybe they're real. (*As she speaks to the child, the Idiot in the corner follows her orders.*) Sleep, boy. Shut your eyes. Tighter. Don't move; stay still or he'll get you. (*She sings.**)

Pretty girl come close the door
A gypsy lad is out before
Your house to take you in your gown
And lead you down to gypsy town.

(*She looks in the mirror.*) They must be gold. (*Like a misbehaving child, the Idiot opens one eye and looks at her.*) Wait till I wear them dancing. (*She tries to hold the mirror back to see more of herself; she fails.*) We get nothing but a little slice of the world and a sliver of broken mirror. But look at my mouth! Just as red as any of the ladies with top-to-toe mirrors and gentlemen who kiss their gloves. (*She looks into the mirror, tries to be refined, fails.*) I'm just a poor slut. That's all. (*The child sits up.*) Shhh, shhh, shhh! Sleep! Close your eyes! Look! (*flashing the mirror against the wall*) It's the sandman! Running across the wall looking for you. (*The Idiot dives out of the darting reflection's way, terrified.*) Eyes tight! (*Marie flashes the mirror in the child's eyes.*) Or he'll stare at your eyes and make you blind! (*Woyzeck enters. Just as the Idiot covers his eyes to keep them from the sandman, Marie sees Woyzeck and covers her ears to hide the earrings.*)

*Music on page 134.

93

WOYZECK
> What have you got?

MARIE
> Nothing.

WOYZECK
> What's in your hand?

MARIE
> Nothing.

WOYZECK
> (*seeing the earring*) What is it?

MARIE
> I found it. An earring.

WOYZECK
> Two of them! That's luck. Never happened to me.

MARIE
> (*sharp*) Aren't I human?

WOYZECK
> Marie, I'm sorry. Look at him sleeping. Perfectly still. Like he's afraid to move and wake himself up. Move his arm; it's pinched. Look at him sweating. Everyone works, everyone sweats. Even in our sleep. Us poor people. Marie, here's some money. My pay and some from the Captain.

MARIE
> Franz — you're — God bless you, Franz.

WOYZECK
> Time to go. Tonight, Marie. I'll see you. (*He goes.*)

MARIE
> I'm a slut. I'm a pig. I could stick a knife in my heart. (*The Idiot looks at her.*) Oh hell, what's the difference? We're all going to hell anyway. The Devil's waiting.

Scene vii

At the Doctor's.

DOCTOR

Woyzeck, I can't believe it. And you call yourself an honest man.

WOYZECK

What's wrong, Doctor sir?

DOCTOR

My eyes are always open, Woyzeck, and I saw it. With these very eyes. You pissed on the street. And you pissed against the wall, like a dog. For that I give you three groschen a day plus meals? Woyzeck, I can't believe it. The world's becoming a bad place, very very bad.

WOYZECK

But Doctor, when nature calls . . .

DOCTOR

What nature? Who nature? What are you talking about? Nature? Did I not prove to you, beyond the ability of even your stupid skull to doubt, that the *musculus constrictor vesicae* can be controlled? Man is free! Choice! Only when we look at humanity can we see deified man's thirst for eternal freedom! And you can't hold your water . . . Did you eat your peas tonight? Peas, only yellow peas. *Cruciferae!* I'm going to unleash a scientific revolution, my boy. I'll blast the lid off the whole works. Urea oxate, ammonium hyperchlorate, hydro-oxydic metabolysis! The day is coming! . . . Woyzeck, couldn't you just go in the other room and try once more to piss?

WOYZECK

I can't, Doctor sir.

DOCTOR

You can't? But you *could* piss all over the wall. I saw it! I made a note of it. I have it here in writing. And remember our contract.

Imagine my horror when I looked out the window, appreciating the yellow sunshine pouring down, and what do I see? There, under the pouring sun, you! Pissing! How could you?... No, now I won't anger myself, Woyzeck. Anger is rage and rage is not calm. Not scientific. Now I am calm, fully calm. My pulse beats at its habitual sixty. I speak in complete sentences. And absolute cold-bloodedness. God forbid that I should anger myself over a man. Now if you were a giant, a god, it might be different — under the right circumstances. But you are just a man . . . Woyzeck, why did you piss on the wall?

WOYZECK

Doctor sir, you see, when a person's a certain kind of person, like if he's made a certain way, then that's his character. But nature's different. Nature's like *that*. (*He snaps his fingers.*) How can I explain it, it's . . .

DOCTOR

Woyzeck, are you philosophizing? Do I pay you three groschen a day to philosophize? If I wanted a philosopher, I'd get a philosopher, wouldn't I?

WOYZECK

Doctor, you know about nature . . .

DOCTOR

Who nature? What nature? Speak up!

WOYZECK

Doctor, do you know about things with double nature? When the sun stops at noon, when the world goes up in fire? And a terrible voice spoke to me.

DOCTOR

Woyzeck, you have an *aberratio*!

WOYZECK

The toadstools, Doctor, it's in the toadstools. Did you ever see the shapes of toadstools when they come up out of the ground? The shapes! The signs! If only I could read them, Doctor . . .

DOCTOR

Woyzeck, you have a magnificent *aberratio mentalis partialis,* secondary classification. Beautifully developed! Your salary is raised, Woyzeck. *Idée fixe* of the highest rank, yet you remain tractable and rational. You do everything as normal? Still shave the Captain?

WOYZECK
Yes, sir.

DOCTOR
Eating your yellow peas?

WOYZECK
Yes, sir. Always, sir. I give the money to my wife.

DOCTOR
Still on duty?

WOYZECK
Yes, sir.

DOCTOR
You're a fascinating case, Woyzeck. Your salary is raised, patient Woyzeck, subject Woyzeck. So behave! Let's feel that pulse. Yes. Ah yes.

Scene viii

In Marie's room.

DRUM MAJOR
Marie!

MARIE
(*as he comes near her*) Come on, let's see you march. Chest like a bull and arms like hammers. There's not a man in the world like you. And no prouder woman.

DRUM MAJOR
> You just wait till dress parade, me in my white plume and white gloves. You've never seen anything like it. When I march by, the Prince says, "That's a real man!"

MARIE
> (*scoffing*) Ha! (*moving to him*) Real man?

DRUM MAJOR
> Christ, we'll plant a whole brood of drum majors. Right?

MARIE
> Get your hands off me.

DRUM MAJOR
> There's hell in your eyes.

MARIE
> What's the difference?

Scene ix

In the street. The Captain runs, panting; he stops and looks around. He has been chasing the Doctor.

CAPTAIN
> Doctor, slow down! Move thoughtfully. You run around like that, you're only chasing death. A man of morals with a clean conscience, a man in your position, never moves that fast. A good man, a man of — (*catching the Doctor by the coat*) Doctor, allow me to save a life.

DOCTOR
> Whose?

CAPTAIN
Mine.

DOCTOR
I'm in a hurry, Captain. No time.

CAPTAIN
(*holding the Doctor*) Doctor, I'm depressed, my mind is depress-ed. I have depressing visions, fantasies, morbid illusions — I break into tears watching my coat hang on a hook.

DOCTOR
Oh you do, do you? I see. Yes. Let me see your neck; stick it out — your neck. Ah. Of course. Thick. Greasy. Constrictive. Apoplec-tic dereliction. Yes, Captain, *apoplexia cerebria* of the head. Total, total. Tsk. But on the other hand you might have it down just one side; you will be paralyzed down just one side. Perhaps you'll be mentally vegetated on just one side — half cabbage and half man. Ah yes. But you might have enough luck to be com-pletely mentally dissolved. You'll sit like a radish for the rest of your days — could be as much as thirty years. What could a radish possibly do for a ghastly stretch of time like that? Hmm. One minute a human being, thinking, talking, whining; the next minute a turnip. Or perhaps an eggplant. A cucumber?

CAPTAIN
Doctor! Please!

DOCTOR
A pickle. Yes. Well, you can expect something like that within the next two-and-a-half weeks — or hours . . .

CAPTAIN
Doctor, you've —

DOCTOR
You'll be a most fascinating case, yes. And if the will of God decrees that just one side of your tongue becomes paralyzed, per-mitting you to say half of each syllable you utter, well then, my good sir, we will conduct the most profound of experiments.

CAPTAIN
Stop trying to scare me. A man can die of fright, you know. Ab-

solute, terror-stricken fright. I've seen it; I've seen it. And there I'll be, lying in state with a frightened expression on my face. I can just see them all, onions up their sleeves, saying "He was a good man, a moral man. We have lost a good man."

DOCTOR
I am teasing you. It is not apoplexy you will die of.

CAPTAIN
Thank the good Lord.

DOCTOR
Not apoplexy at all. No, no . . . (*Woyzeck rushes past.*)

CAPTAIN
Woyzeck! Halt! Hold it! Where are you going so fast? Rushing through the world like a razor, you could cut someone. Woyzeck, why do I think of beards whenever I see you? It's morbid, it's not healthy. Doctor, I've got to talk to you about this.

DOCTOR
As Pliny points out, long beards worn upon the face is a pleasure impermissible to platoon soldiers.

CAPTAIN
If that's a reflection on me, sir—

DOCTOR
Not at all, sir. You have no beard.

CAPTAIN
So I don't. But there are those who do, eh, Woyzeck? Any beard hairs in your porridge bowl? You get my meaning, Woyzeck?

WOYZECK
No sir, Captain sir, I don't.

CAPTAIN
Beard hairs! Facial pilosity!

DOCTOR
(*commenting on the Captain's choice of word*) Remarkable.

CAPTAIN
Thank you. Hair from the face of a — a general, maybe? Or a sergeant? No? Maybe from — a — drum major? Eh? Well,

Woyzeck? What do you say? But you've got a moral wife, my boy; a good, moral woman. Not like the others.

WOYZECK

Sir, I don't understand, Captain sir.

CAPTAIN

Ah! Look at that face, Doctor. Well, perhaps not in his porridge bowl, but perhaps on a pair of lips? Lips, Woyzeck, lips! I know about those things. I know about love, Woyzeck. Look at him, Doctor. He's turned white.

WOYZECK

Captain sir, I've — I'm not much of anything, sir — I — there isn't anything else, sir; I don't have anything else but her, not in the world, sir. Captain sir, if you're just kidding me —

CAPTAIN

I? A commissioned officer? Kid? Woyzeck!

DOCTOR

Woyzeck, your pulse. Abrupt! Choppy! Irregular! Strange.

WOYZECK

Captain, it's hot, this earth, like the fires of hell. But I feel cold, I feel the cold, Captain. Ice. Hell is freezing. Want to bet? I'll bet. Captain, I don't believe you. Lord God, I can't believe it!

CAPTAIN

Listen, you! Who do you think you're — you want a bullet in your brain? You stand there cutting into me with your eyes — I'm just trying to help, Woyzeck. Because you're good, Woyzeck, a moral man.

DOCTOR

Facial muscles tense, unmoving, tight. Occasional twitch. Condition tense, tight, unpredictable. Fascinating!

WOYZECK

Anything can happen, Captain. Anything. Marie! What can't happen? It's nice today, Captain. The weather. The sky is gray, glossy, hard. A man could pound a spike in and hang himself from it. And just for the space between yes and the second yes and

no. Captain! Yes and no! Is yes because there's no? Or no because
of yes? Captain? I've got to think about that, I've got to think
about that. (*He runs off.*)

DOCTOR

(*shouting after him*) Amazing! (*to the Captain*) A laboratory
phenomenon. (*after Woyzeck*) Woyzeck! You get another raise!

CAPTAIN

People like that make my brain spin around. I get dizzy watching
him go. Faster and faster, faster and faster. Like a spider running
away from its shadow. But a good man can take care of himself,
Doctor. A good man has to take care of himself: a good man can't
have courage. Only pigs have courage. Only pig bitches. That's
why I'm in the army — because I have no courage. Look at him.
He's gone already. Grotesque! Grotesque!

Scene x

In Marie's room.

WOYZECK

(*looking at her*) Why can't I see it? God, it's there, why can't I see
it? Why can't I crush it in my fists?

MARIE

Franz! You're delirious, Franz.

WOYZECK

So huge, so bulging — a sin to squeeze the angels into hell. Marie,
your mouth's so red! No sores there, Marie? Marie! You're
beautiful — like a sin. How can sin be so beautiful?

MARIE

It's your fever, Franz.

WOYZECK

Why wasn't it me? Did he stand here? This way? Like this?

MARIE

It's an old world and a long day and anyone can stand any place.

WOYZECK

Lots of people walk on that street, don't they, Marie? It's nice to walk the street, to be out there in society. And Marie talks to society, doesn't she? But that's none of my business.

MARIE

Should I tell people to stay off the street? Should I say I've got no mouth and can't talk to them?

WOYZECK

You've got a mouth, Marie. (*He picks up the piece of broken mirror.*) Look at it! Don't ever forget your mouth. Beautiful lips, Marie. Keep the flies off them.

MARIE

What fly stung you?

WOYZECK

I saw.

MARIE

You're like a cow chased by hornets.

WOYZECK

I saw!

MARIE

Lots of people with two eyes see while the sun's out.

WOYZECK

Whore! (*He moves toward her.*)

MARIE

Stay away from me, Franz. I'd rather feel a knife in my stomach than your hands. From the day I was ten my father couldn't touch me when I looked at him.

WOYZECK

(*close to hitting her*) Whore! Why can't I see it? There's nothing in your eyes. How are you hiding it? Your eyes are like a well; I get dizzy looking down them — and there's nothing to see but innocence. But there's dirt there. Even if I can't prove it. I can't touch it. Who can prove it?

Scene xi

At the sentry-house.

ANDRE
(*singing**)
Our hostess has a pretty girl
Sitting in her garden day by day . . .
WOYZECK
Andre!
ANDRE
What?
WOYZECK
(*pause*) Good weather.
ANDRE
Sunday weather. There'll be music out there tonight. The whores're there, the men're already stinking. Lovely night.
WOYZECK
Do you hear them dancing?
ANDRE
Yeah. It's not me, what do I care? (*He sings.*)
Sitting, sitting in her garden day by day
Till twelve church bells have tolled away,
And the infantry comes marching . . .

*Music on page 135.

WOYZECK
  Andre, I can't stay here.
ANDRE
  You have to.
WOYZECK
  It's twisting in front of my eyes, inside my head. They're dancing.
  Her hands will be hot, Andre; do you know what that means?
ANDRE
  What's the matter?
WOYZECK
  Dancing. I've got to go there. I've got to see.
ANDRE
  Why? Sit down. She's a whore. You said so already. So forget it.
  What's one more whore?
WOYZECK
  It's too hot. I've got to go. (*He leaves.*)

Scene xii

At the inn.

FIRST APPRENTICE
  (*singing**)
    My stinking shirt, it is not mine.
    Like my soul it stinks of brandywine.
SECOND APPRENTICE
  Brother! Allow that I prove my friendship by punching a hole in
  your nature. Onwards! I'm gonna knock a hole right in his nature.
  Shit, I'm big as him.

*Music on page 135.

FIRST APPRENTICE

My soul, my soul: it stinketh. Brandywine doth render my soul
stunken. BUT even golden money passeth unto rot, and Decay
thus tightens her purse. Remember me, for it was beautiful in the
world. (*crying*) It was, it was. Brother, my tears fall like the
saddest brandywine, like rain — let me fill the barrel with tears.
Oh, that our noses were decanters, and we could pour them down
each other's throats!

ALL

(*singing**)

> *A huntsman from the big river*
> *Galloped past the forest of trees*
> *As free and high as the meadow*
> *It's the hunter's life for me!*
>
> *Hallo hallo he called to me,*
> *Hallo hallo he called!*
> *As free and high as the meadow*
> *It's the hunter's life for me!*

(*Woyzeck appears outside. Marie dances by with the Drum Major, not seeing Woyzeck.*)

WOYZECK

There! God damn her.

MARIE

Faster! Don't stop! Faster! Faster!

WOYZECK

(*sitting in the doorway, shaking*) Hear! Hear them! Spin! Twirl!
Roll, roll, roll on each other. Turn and roll. Don't stop, never
stop.

IDIOT

(*with Woyzeck*) The stench — acchh!

WOYZECK

Yes, her cheeks! The stench! They're red, still full of blood — why
does she stink already? Karl, what do you smell?

*Music on page 135.

IDIOT

Stench! Stench! Blood?

WOYZECK

Blood? Everything I look at is red. Why, Karl?

IDIOT

Blood.

WOYZECK

Look at them, tossing, rolling, turning in a sea of blood, one over the other, one under the other. (*in fright*) Ah! The sea is red, red . . . Don't stop, stop, stop — (*beating his fists together*) Spin, twirl, roll, don't stop, roll on each other, roll, roll, roll, roll, roll . . . GOD! Crush out the sun so they can roll in their slime. Human and man and man and woman. Human and human and male and female and woman and beast. Right in the heat of the sun! They'll do it in the light of the day. They do it on the flat of your hand like flies. Hot as coal, red as lips. Don't stop. It's cold, don't stop. Whore! Look how he grabs at her! Look at his hands in her flesh. Her body, he's touching it in his fingers, he's holding where I touched, where I held . . . (*He collapses.*)

FIRST APPRENTICE

Listen unto me while I sayeth unto thee, do ye not neglect the pilgrim pressing past the sweep of time, for he answereth himself as with the learning of God, and sayeth, "Man. What man? What is man?" And truly I spake to ye and thee, and questeth: How should the plowman, the smith, the cobbler, the doctor live, were man not here for their use? Could there be modesty without tailors? Could there be soldiers had not God granted man the right to butcher himself? Therefore doubt not but that all there is, is lovely and sweetly. For the world and the things of the world decay, and even money rotteth. In conclusion, brothers of my brethren, suck deep the draught to better piss again on the cross of the Lord, so that somewhere a Jew can die. (*Woyzeck awakens amid music, singing, and dancing.*)

ANDRE

Why are you here?

WOYZECK
What time is it?

ANDRE
Around ten.

WOYZECK
Only ten? Make it go faster. I've got to think about it soon.

ANDRE
What?

WOYZECK
The fun.

ANDRE
Why?

WOYZECK
So it'll be over.

ANDRE
Why are you sitting in the doorway?

WOYZECK
It feels nice.

ANDRE
You're drunk.

WOYZECK
Anybody can sit in doors, but nobody knows — not till they're hauled off feet first.

IDIOT
(*waking with a start*) Where?!

ANDRE
Come on.

WOYZECK
I've got to lie down.

ANDRE
You've got blood on your head.

IDIOT
Stench.

WOYZECK
In, in, *in* my head! Look at them. If they knew about the clock

they'd rip off their clothes, put a black tie on, and white powder,
and tell the carpenter to make their beds.

ANDRE

(*to the Idiot*) He's drunk. (*Andre leaves.*)

WOYZECK

Something broke the world. The chimney sweep forgot to sweep
my eyes. It's dark. God damn you, God. Devils! (*People leave,
climbing over him in the doorway.*) I'm right in my own way. Hop
myself over myself. Hip-hop! Hippity-hop! What happened to
my shadow? Nobody runs a decent kennel around here. Where's
the moon? Christ! Shine it through my legs so I can find my
shadow. (*He rolls himself over so the moon can shine between his
legs from behind. He sings.**)

> Gnawing along the green green lawn
> Gnawing along the green green lawn
> Till the lawn was gone from the ground — oh.

(*still looking at the moon*) What's that? Sparkling! It's pulling my
eyes out. Shine, shine. Look at it, let go, I've got to have it. (*He
rushes off.*)

Scene xiii

In an open field.

WOYZECK

Don't stop! Don't stop! Shhhhhhhhaaahhhhh! Wwwisshhhh!
That's the fiddles and horns. Shhhhhhwhishh. Don't stop, don't
stop — enough music. Quiet! I hear it! Something — there —

*Music on page 134.

(*pointing to the ground*) What? Louder! I can't hear! Yell it! Scream it at me! Stab? Stab? Stick the goatbitch dead? Stab her? Dead? Should I? Must I? Scream it! I have to hear. What? Is it there too? And here? The words won't stop. Make the wind drown it out, scream, break the ground apart — still there? Stab? The wind's howling: stab, stick the pigbitch dead. (*silence*)

Scene xiv

In the barracks.

WOYZECK

(*softly*) Andre. (*Andre mutters in his sleep. Woyzeck shakes him.*) Andre. Andre!

ANDRE

What?

WOYZECK

I can't sleep. When my eyes are closed, everything turns and spins. And the fiddles talk: don't stop, don't stop. And the walls, too. How can you sleep?

ANDRE

Well, so let 'em dance. So what? What's one more dance? I gotta sleep.

WOYZECK

I keep hearing it: stab. I put my hands over my ears and when I close my eyes there's a black silence, and it shines there in front of me, hanging, floating, a long flat knife. Like a razor. Behind a window in a dark, dirty street — and an old man's eyes, looking, seeing me. I keep seeing it, I —

ANDRE
 I want to go to sleep.
WOYZECK
 Andre! Listen! Something's out there. Under the ground. Listen,
 can't you hear them? They're under the bed, they're pounding
 under the floor. It's loud, so loud. Don't stop; stab, don't stop —
ANDRE
 Shh!

Scene xv

In the Doctor's courtyard. The Doctor is on a high balcony.

DOCTOR
 Students! Like David on first seeing Bathsheba, I stand upon the
 roof. But I see no Bathsheba. I see instead the bloomers of the
 girls' school drying on a line — and it is this that leads me to the
 object of our subject for today: the grave matter of the
 relationship of the subject to the object. For example, were I to
 take one of those (*indicating the bloomers*) delightful things in
 which we sometimes find the most magnificent manifestations of
 the obviousness of the spiritually and divinely theological, and
 carefully prod through it, scrutinizing it for its connections with
 the world, space, the galaxies in general, and nature — Students,
 if I toss this ball from this height, *nature* dictates that it will fall!
 Note how its *centrum gravitationis* descends with all the rest of it.
 Remarkable, is it not, my students? Right, Woyzeck? (*He
 screams.*) WOYZECK!!

WOYZECK
Doctor, I feel sick.

DOCTOR
Why are you standing there so precariously? You're not your grandmother.

WOYZECK
I can't stop shaking.

DOCTOR
(*descending, delighted*) Wonderful, Woyzeck, fine! Gentlemen! Look here! As the ball falls as a result of its nature, look, just look at this man here. For months he's been fed only peas, nothing but peas. And in spite of everything, look! Examine him! Examine! (*They all examine him.*) Feel his erratic pulse! *Try* to find his blood pressure.

WOYZECK
Doctor, everything's dark, everything's getting—

DOCTOR
Courage, Woyzeck. It'll all be over soon. Feel the pulse, students; feel, will you? Before it's too late.

WOYZECK
I'm dizzy, Doctor sir . . .

DOCTOR
Which reminds me — Woyzeck, make your ears wiggle for the students. Students, he wiggles his ears — both of them — with just a single muscle! Come on, will you? What do you think I pay you for? Ah! There! Good, do you see, students? You are witnessing the actual transmortification of a human being into a donkey. It is a severe and common malady, brought about through being brought up by women and speaking German. Woyzeck! Your hair's thinning out! Has your sentimental old mother been yanking at it for a keepsake of you? I can see your skull, Woyzeck — right through your skin. It's the yellow peas, gentlemen! It's all in the peas.

Scene xvi

At the inn.

WOYZECK

(*singing**)

> *Daughter, oh my daughter,*
> *Take a word now from a friend:*
> *Hanging round*
> *The stable ground*
> *With stable boys*
> *And stable men*
> *Will lead to no good end, my girl;*
> *Will lead to no good end.*

(*speaking*) What can't be done? What cannot be done, even by God? What even God cannot do is to undo what He has done. And that's how it is. Yet still, improvement is improvement. A virtuous man loves life, and a man who loves life is a coward. Only pigs have courage.

SERGEANT

(*with dignity*) You are in the presence of a brave man.

WOYZECK

Was I talking to you? I wasn't talking to you. Still, it was good of you to listen. Only pigs have courage.

SERGEANT

Listen, you. Be careful. Or I'll make you drink a pail of your own piss and choke you on your razor.

WOYZECK

Sir! You insult yourself. Was I talking about you? Was I talking *to* you? Did I say *you* have courage? Don't confuse me, good man. I am science. My name is science. My weekly wage for my scien-

*Music on page 135.

113

tific occupation is one guilder. Cut me in half and I'll starve. I'm a *spinosa pericyclis*: even my ass has a Latin name. I am a skeleton — alive, breathing. A phenomenon. Mankind scrutinizes me, mankind studies Franz Woyzeck, scientist. Man! What man? What is man? Dirt, dust, dung. Stupid mankind, stupid dirt, stupid dust, stupid dung. Some dung is more stupid than other dirt . . . Let us be friends. If we could be friends there could be no science. Just nature. Don't articulate. Don't amputate. What's this here? Dung! Why? Why dung? Stupid dung! Ah, my friend, man is dung, man is man, man loves man. His own kind. He beats, he shoots, he stabs his own kind. He beats, he shoots, he stabs dung. Why? Like babies doing mudpies on a stable floor . . . (*sobbing*) We are friends. I wish our noses were decanters to pour down our throats. Ah, this is a place! Beauty, good friend. Look! The clouds part and the sun pours through — like God's bedpan emptying onto the world.

Scene xvii

In the barracks yard.

WOYZECK
Hear anything?
ANDRE
He's inside.
WOYZECK
What's he saying?
ANDRE
Nothing. He's not saying anything. (*pause*) Why me? How come I

have to tell you? (*pause*) All right. He was laughing. Then he said
she was hot as a pistol. Then he said — uh — something about her
thighs. And she moves like a — I forget.

WOYZECK
So that's what you heard? I dreamed last night, Andre. What
stupid things people dream. A dream about a knife. Stupid.
(*Woyzeck starts off.*)

ANDRE
Where are you going?

WOYZECK
The Captain wants his wine. He can't live through the morning
without his wine. Andre? You know what? Everything's calm. I
feel like I'm rolling over in bed on Sunday morning. There's hardly any girls like she was.

ANDRE
What?

WOYZECK
Never mind.

Scene xviii

At the inn.

DRUM MAJOR
(*drunk*) I'm a man! (*He pounds his chest.*) You hear? Someone
say different? Anyone who's not drunk as God Himself better
drink. Or he'll find his head up his butt — shoved there by me. I'll
— (*to Woyzeck*) Hey! (*Woyzeck looks at him but says nothing.*)
Hey! You! Yes, you. I'm looking straight at you and I'm talking.

If you were drunk, you'd know I'm talking to you. (*no response*)
Drink, you son of a bitch. Have a drink. (*Woyzeck waves the
offer away. The Drum Major grabs Woyzeck.*) I say drink, you
drink, you hear? (*He shoves Woyzeck away; Woyzeck sits again.
The Drum Major wobbles back to his seat. He looks back at
Woyzeck.*) Not drinking yet? (*He grabs Woyzeck again and
throws him savagely to the floor.*) You're lucky I leave you
enough wind for an old lady's fart. (*Woyzeck remains shaking on
the floor.*) Aaaaaah, what the hell do I care? Don't drink. Son of a
bitch. (*The Drum Major sings.**)
> *Life is in brandy, brandy, brandy;*
> *It bites my brain and makes me brave.*

A MAN
Took care of him, all right.
ANOTHER MAN
He's bleeding.
WOYZECK
One thing after another.

Scene xix

In a pawnshop.

WOYZECK
I don't have enough for the pistol.
JEW
So? So you won't be a sharpshooter.

*Music on page 136.

WOYZECK
How about the knife?

JEW
Good knife. Sharp. What are you going to do with it, cut your throat? It's sharp enough. Don't worry about it. It's as cheap here as any place. You can die cheap. But it's gotta cost something — two groschen.

WOYZECK
(*holding the knife*) It'll slice more than bread.

JEW
So? So three groschen then. (*Woyzeck puts the money on the counter and leaves.*) Look at that! Throws it down like it was nothing. Without a word. (*He bites it.*) And it's real.

Scene xx

In Marie's room.

IDIOT
(*to the child*) This one is golden-crown. He is my lord his king the highness. Tomorrow I'll show you my lady her highness the queen. Then after that her prince, her child . . . see? Liversausage yells at Bloodsausage: "Shut up, Bloodsausage!" And Bloodsausage, he says — he doesn't say anything, because he's Bloodsausage, and he doesn't have to say anything.

MARIE
(*reading*) "And no guile is found in his mouth." My God, don't look down at me. (*turning pages*) "And the scribes and Pharisees

brought unto Him a woman taken in adultery, and set her in the midst. . . . And Jesus said unto her, 'Neither do I condemn thee: go, and sin no more.' " My God, my God, make me strong enough to pray. Please let me. (*looking at the child*) Child, you rest in my heart like a knife. (*to the Idiot*) Karl! I've flaunted, like a whore, like the whore I am, under the sun . . . sin, to sin in the light of the sun, Karl, do you know? Do you know? (*The Idiot moves away with the child, singing a bit of the wordless lullaby.**) Franz didn't come today. Or yesterday. He's not here. He — it's getting hot in here. (*She reads.*) ". . . and stood at His feet weeping, and began to wash His feet with tears, and did wipe them with the hairs of her head, and anointed them with ointment." It's all broken. Everything is dead. Christ! My Christ! Let *me* anoint your feet . . .

Scene xxi

In an open field.

WOYZECK

(*alone, burying the knife*) Thou shalt not kill. Thou shalt not kill. Thou shalt not kill.

*Music on page 134.

Scene xxii

In the barracks. Woyzeck rummages through his belongings. Andre is crying.

WOYZECK

Andre, this isn't a uniform jacket. But maybe you could wear it anyway. This is my sister's cross. And her ring. And there's a holy picture here. Of two hearts. I think they're solid gold, from my mother's Bible. It says, "Lord, Thy body, nailed and broken: My heart shall be Thy body's token." My mother doesn't feel anything any more, except when the sun warms her hands. Well, so what? So what? (*reading a document*) Name: Friedrich Johann Franz Woyzeck. Rank: Private. Rifleman, Second Regiment, Second Battalion, Company Four. Date of birth: March the twenty-fifth, the Feast of the Annunciation. Today is the day, Andre; today I am twenty-four years, eight months, and sixteen days old. And hours and minutes.

ANDRE

Go to the hospital. They'll give you something to kill the fever.

WOYZECK

(*shoving all his stuff toward Andre*) Here, Andre. When the carpenter builds his box, there's no way to know who it's for.

Scene xxiii

*In the street. The Idiot claps time as a small girl sings a song.**

GIRL

> *On Candlemas Day the sun in the sky*
> *And the corn were yellow as gold.*
> *The soldiers marched with their heads held high*
> *And the road they marched was old.*

> *The fiddlers stepped behind and were led*
> *By the pipers and drums and bells;*
> *And the leggings they wore were blood scarlet red,*
> *And their . . .*

MARIE

(*interrupting*) I don't like that song.

GIRL

(*to an old woman*) Grandmother, tell a story.

GRANDMOTHER

All right, you little crab apple. Once upon a time there was a little girl with no father and no mother. They were dead. Everyone was dead, everyone in the whole wide world was dead. So the poor little girl went out looking for someone. But everyone was dead. So she decided to go up to heaven. The moon looked down, smiling at her, and she climbed — but when she got to the moon, it was a piece of rotten wood. So she kept going till she got to the sun, and it was a dried-out sunflower. And when she went on to the stars, they were little gold flies, stuck up there like in a spider web. So she went back down to the earth, but it was an upside-down flowerpot. So she sat down all alone and cried. And even to this very day she sits and cries all alone, all all alone. (*It has become dark during the Grandmother's last words. The remainder of this scene is played in darkness.*)

*Music on page 136.

120

WOYZECK
> (*appearing*) Marie.

MARIE
> (*frightened*) What?

WOYZECK
> It's time. Let's go.

MARIE
> Where?

WOYZECK
> How do I know?

Scene xxiv

At the pond.

MARIE
> It's dark here, Franz. Which way is town?

WOYZECK
> Sit down, Marie.

MARIE
> I've got to go back.

WOYZECK
> What for, Marie? Sit down. Your feet will get sore. (*He pulls her down.*)

MARIE
> Franz, what's the matter with you?

WOYZECK
> How long has it been, Marie?

MARIE

    Two years.

WOYZECK

    From Pentecost.

MARIE

    From Pentecost.

WOYZECK

    How much longer will it be, Marie?

MARIE

    Franz, I've got to go. I have to make supper . . .

WOYZECK

    Are you cold, Marie? But I can feel how warm you are — even if I
    don't touch you. You have lips like hot coals. Hotter: the breath
    of a whore. I'd still give up heaven to kiss them again. Cold,
    Marie? But when you're cold all the way through, you'll be warm.
    The morning dew won't be cold.

MARIE

    What do you mean?

WOYZECK

    Nothing. (*silence*)

MARIE

    The moon's coming up. Look how red it is.

WOYZECK

    Like blood on a knife. Marie, I love you. (*He stabs her. When she
    is dead, he moves away from her body. He stops some distance
    away, listens, and looks down at the ground.*) Say something! (*He
    falls to the ground, beating it with his fists.*) Damn you damn you
    damn you damn you . . .

Scene xxv

At the inn. The inn is crowded; there's music, drinking, and dancing. Kathy is the most prominent of the dancers. Woyzeck staggers in; everything stops. Silently everyone stares at Woyzeck in the doorway. In an attempt to restore the mood Woyzeck tries to sing.*

WOYZECK

> *Daughter, oh my daughter,*
> *Take a word now from a friend:*
> *Hanging round*
> *The stable ground*
> *With stable boys*
> *And stable men*
> *Will get you in the end, my girl;*
> *Will get you in the end — oh.*

(*dead silence*) Hey! Everybody drink! Everybody drink! Don't stop! Sweat and stink; he'll get everyone in the end. (*Dead silence; all watch him.*) You! Kathy! Come here! Sit. (*He pulls the girl onto his lap.*) It's hot, Kathy, can you feel it? Here, Kathy, here . . . (*He leans her back, kisses her, feels her body.*) That's how it is! The devil takes some, lets others get away. You, Kathy, you're too hot to touch. Here, Kathy, here . . . (*He touches her.*) Kathy, lovely lady, you'll be cold as cold coals someday. Do you know that, Kathy? Cold as clay. (*Kathy tries to get up. He pulls her back. She looks around for help; no one moves.*) Relax, girl. Sing something, Kathy. Sing!

KATHY

> (*singing, both annoyed and afraid**)
> *In Swabia I'll never be*
> *And dresses long are not for me.*
> *For dresses long and shoes that shine*
> *For girls like me are far too fine.*

*Music on pages 135 and 136.

WOYZECK

No shoes! Not one shoe! Right, Kathy. We'll get to hell barefoot.

KATHY

(*singing*)
> *Put your dresses and shoes back on the shelf;*
> *Take back your wine and do it yourself.*

(*That breaks the tension. There is laughter from the men, including Woyzeck. The general merriment starts again.*)

WOYZECK

My hands won't stop touching you, Kathy. They crawl on you like they've escaped.

KATHY

(*startled*) There's blood on your hand.

WOYZECK

My hand?

KATHY

Now it's on my dress. You got it on my dress. There's blood.

WOYZECK

Blood? Blood?

INNKEEPER

That's what it looks like.

IDIOT

Stench! Acchh!

WOYZECK

I cut myself. Right here, my right hand, see?

INNKEEPER

Your right hand? Then why's there blood on your elbow?

WOYZECK

I wiped it off my hand . . .

INNKEEPER

Blood on your right hand and you wiped it off with your right elbow? That's pretty good.

IDIOT

But suddenly the giant said,
"I feel a thought inside my head.
Fee, fie, fum, fam,
My nose can smell the blood of man!"
Phew. It's already stink.

WOYZECK

So what? What do you care? Look out. Move, stay away from me.
Anyone who comes near me, I'll — damn! What are you staring
at? Do I look like a killer? You should see your*selves*. Look at
you. Look out. Out of my way! (*He runs off. The Idiot follows,
imitating Woyzeck's run.*)

IDIOT

Hip-hop. Hippity-hop. Hip-hop. Hippity-hop.

Scene xxvi

At the pond.

WOYZECK

What did I do with the knife? (*in a strange voice*) Woyzeck, go
back, Woyzeck, find the knife; they'll know it was you. Here, over
here, near here ... (*He stumbles over Marie's body.*) What's that?
Ah! Marie! (*He kneels by the body.*) Marie, what are you doing
out here? Sweating, Marie? Stinking? You're wet, Marie, wet and
warm. (*looking at the blood on his fingers*) And it's so quiet.

Marie, why are you pale? Where did you get that red necklace; who strung those red beads around your neck? Did you sin for those beads, Marie? Are they real? Marie, your sins were black and I made you pale, I made you white. And you didn't comb your hair. Where is it? The knife — ah, here! (*He throws the knife into the pond. In the distance the Idiot is heard singing the wordless lullaby.*) There! Into the pond, like a stone into a well. They won't find it — but maybe when they swim in the summer — (*He goes into the pond.*) Here. (*He throws the knife farther out.*) There! It'll rust. They'll never find it. Ah, ah, I should have taken it away from here, they might — they might — (*in terror*) There's blood on my hand! Wash it away, Woyzeck. No blood left on you. Here, another spot, wash it off, another spot — spot — spot . . . (*He disappears into the pond. The Idiot enters with the child, still quietly singing.*)

IDIOT

Water, water, he's in the water. Wet as water in the water. Ho, boy! Hip-hop! (*He sees the xody.*) Hip-hop. Hippity-hop. Hip-hop. (*He sings the lullaby again. The Police Chief enters with several townspeople. They contemplate the body for a long time.*)

POLICE CHIEF

(*impressed and awed*) Now that's what I call a murder. Absolutely genuine, real live murder! You know how long it's been since I've seen one like this? (*The lights fade to end the play; the Idiot's singing continues into the blackness.*)

Production History

This adaptation of *Woyzeck* was first produced in March 1972 at Theatre 1900 in Minneapolis under the direction of David Ball. A second production followed at the Chimera Theatre in St. Paul.

Original Cast

Woyzeck . . . . John Martin
Captain . . . . Clint Knudson
Andre . . . . Stuart Franklin
Marie . . . . Valery Daemke
Idiot . . . . Warren Bowles
Margret . . . . Mary Beth Cecka
Drum Major . . . . Joel Brooks
Old Man . . . . Jean-Paul Mustone
Charlatan . . . . Roger Bulington
Sergeant . . . . Michael Rockne
Proprietor . . . . Dan McDonough
Doctor . . . . Jean-Paul Mustone
First Apprentice . . . . Roger Bulington
Second Apprentice . . . . Tom Krueger
Jew . . . . Joel Brooks
Girl . . . . Pam Madson
Grandmother . . . . Holly Herbig
Kathy . . . . Mary Beth Cecka
Police Chief . . . . Clint Knudson
Musicians . . . . David Campbell, Terry Dunn,
Julie Powell
Townspeople . . . . Barbara Haglund, Tracy Knudson,
Vickie Madson, Cheryl Salo,
Ramona Shaw, Virginia Shaw

Music composed by Susan Hesse Keller
Choreography by Lupi Nehls

John Martin as Woyzeck; Stuart Franklin as Andre. (Photograph by Lynn Ball.)

Above, Valery Daemke as Marie; *below,* John Martin as Woyzeck. (Photograph by Lynn Ball.)

Valery Daemke as Marie. (Photograph by Lynn Ball.)

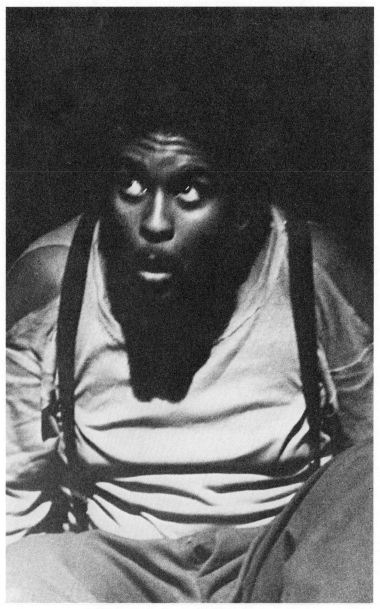

Warren Bowles as the Idiot. (Photograph by Lynn Ball.)

Two Rabbits (unaccompanied)

Two rab-bits sat in the deep-est grass, Gnaw-ing a-long the green, green lawn...

Gnaw-ing a-long the green, green lawn 'til the lawn was gone from the ground.

Lullaby (hummed, unaccompanied)

Old Man's Song (unaccompanied)

Slowly, sadly No-thing on this earth can last, Life is like the sum-mer grass, The

world's too fast, too fast, Too fast...

Marie's Song (unaccompanied)

Pret-ty maid come close the door, A gyp-sy lad is out be-fore your

house to take you in your gown And lead you down to gyp-sy town.

Andre's Song (with guitar)

Our hos-tess has a pret-ty girl, Sit-ting in her gar-den day by day; Til twelve church bells have tolled a-way, And the in-fan-try comes mar-ching.

First Apprentice's Song (unaccompanied)

Drunkenly My stin-king shirt, It is not mine; Like my soul it stinks of bran-dy-wine...

The Huntsman (with improvised piano, providing solid rhythm)

Robustly A hunts-man from the big ri-ver gal-loped past the for-est of trees; As free and high as the mea-dow, It's the hun-ter's life for me. Hal-lo, hal-lo, he called to me, hal-lo, hal-lo he called; As free and high as the mea-dow, It's the hun-ter's life for me.

No Good End (sung unaccompanied)

Daughter, oh my daugh-ter, take a word now from a friend: Hang-ing round the sta-ble grounds with sta-ble boys and sta-ble men Will lead to no good end, my girl, Will lead to no good end.

Brandy, Brandy *(unaccompanied)*

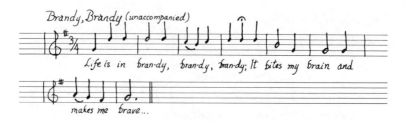

Life is in bran-dy, bran-dy, bran-dy; It bites my brain and

makes me brave...

Child's Song *(unaccompanied)*

1. On Can-dle-mas Day the sun in the sky And the corn were yel-low as
2. The fid-dlers stepped be-hind and were led By the pipers and drums and

gold; The sol-diers marched with their heads held high and the road they marched was old.
bells; And the leggings they wore were blood scar-let red, And their...

Kathy's Song *(unaccompanied)*

In Swa-bi-a I'll ne-ver be, And dres-ses long are not for me, For

dres-ses long and shoes that shine For girls like me are far too fine. Put your

dres-ses and shoes back on the shelf, Take back your wine and do it your-self.

Fables Here and Then

Created by David Feldshuh
with members of the Guthrie Theater company

For Kiki

The playlets in *Fables Here and Then* have been adapted with the permission of the publishers from stories in copyrighted volumes: *How the Snake Lost His Voice, The Silver Bell,* and *The Fisherman and the Sea King's Daughter* from *Fairy Tales from Japan* by Miroslav Novak, translated by Alice Denesova (© copyright 1970 by Artia; published by The Hamlyn Publishing Group Limited, London); *Gassir the Hero* from *African Tales of Magic and Mystery,* retold by Maria Kosova and Vladislav Stanovsky, translated by Olga Kuthanova (© copyright 1970 by Artia; published by The Hamlyn Publishing Group Limited, London, for Golden Pleasure Books Limited); *The Indians and Death* from *American Indian Tales and Legends* by Vladimir Hulpach, translated by George Theiner (© copyright 1965 by Artia; published by Paul Hamlyn, London, for Golden Pleasure Books Limited); *The Suicide* and *The Gas Company* from *True Stories* by Christopher Logue (© 1967 by Christopher Logue; first published by New English Library, London, now available in a new edition from André Deutsch, London).

The lyrics for "Side by Side" by Harry Woods are used with the permission of the publisher: © Copyright MCMXXVII by Shapiro, Bernstein & Co., Inc., 10 East 53rd Street, New York, New York 10022; copyright renewed and assigned to Shapiro, Bernstein & Co., Inc. The lyrics for "Gassir the Hero" were adapted by David Ball.

Information about performance rights may be obtained from Donald Schoenbaum, The Guthrie Theater, 725 Vineland Place, Minneapolis, Minnesota 55403.

The author would like to thank Carmelita DiMichael and Nancy Miller for their encouragement and assistance in preparing *Fables Here and Then* for publication.

Comments

When Michael Langham became the artistic director of The Guthrie Theater, one of his major goals was to extend its resources throughout the Midwest. As part of this effort, I was approached in the spring of 1971 and asked if there was anything I wanted to direct that might be appropriate for a three-month tour beginning that fall. The play had to have a small cast, a minimum of sets and costumes, and content that would appeal on many levels to people of all ages. For most of our audience it would be their first contact with us, and we needed something that would be warm and friendly while at the same time totally professional.

I decided to create an original production using "story theater" techniques. I had seen Paul Sills's *Story Theater* on Broadway and was fascinated with the form. It seemed to offer exciting opportunities to explore the various physical aspects of acting with which I had been experimenting for a number of years: mime, karate, stage fighting, and concentration exercises. I set about searching for the most theatrical material I could find. After reading some 250 tales, legends, myths, and anecdotes, I stumbled onto the beautifully illustrated Hamlyn publications from which the majority of the stories in *Fables Here and Then* were taken. I tried to choose stories that were exciting, that would translate successfully to the stage, and that would balance each other and give the show variety.

I felt that the production had to be an ensemble work — no stars, or better, everyone a star. I also wanted the show to be very physical, to

139

have the actors display a wide range of theatrical talents individually and collectively, and to have the whole evening radiate a warm "let's pretend" innocence. (The multiple roles — animate and inanimate — assigned to the actors are indicated in the chart on pages 150-151.)

I selected six young actors — Ross Bickell, Ivar Brogger, Lance Davis, Tovah Feldshuh, Katherine Ferrand, and Erik Fredricksen — and asked Roberta Carlson to do the music. David Hawkanson agreed to arrange and manage the tour. We launched headfirst into three hundred hours of rehearsal: playing games, portraying animals, improvising stories, singing, tap-dancing, doing karate, tumbling, stick fighting, and practicing mime. It was tedious at times and often very difficult, but a lot of laughter carried us through. My most important advice to anyone who directs *Fables* is that in order to work the final product must convey exuberance, humanity, and joy. It will not be there in performance if it is not there in rehearsal.

After working for a week on storytelling, we reached the conclusion that physicalization is the essential ingredient that must be added to a story in bringing it to the stage. We used a number of exercises in learning to physicalize a story. Several of these were taken from Viola Spolin's immensely valuable book *Improvisation for the Theater* (Northwestern University Press, 1963).

Exercise 1. The actor tells a story.

Exercise 2. The actor repeats the story, trying this time to convey all the essential details while pretending that the audience is deaf. (See Spolin's "Deaf Audience" exercise.) This forces the actor to physicalize as much as possible and to make visual that which was previously communicated through spoken language.

Exercise 3. The actor pantomimes the story. For our purposes pantomime is best understood as the substitution of a gesture for a word. It is a type of sign language, and in this exercise *every* word that can possibly be physicalized should be. Pantomime is also important in helping the actors to understand the relationship between narrator and character in story theater. For example, the script might read: "I speak. You listen. Over here is a conductor. Over here is a violinist.

The conductor conducts. The violinist plays. The conductor says, 'Watch my rhythm.' The violinist replies, 'You're conducting too fast.'" This could be pantomimed as follows:

(a)   I speak. You listen. (*The actor faces his audience and substitutes a gesture for each word in the phrase. For example, he points to himself, he points to his mouth, he points to a member of the audience, he cups his ears with his hands. His audience is now quiet and focused on him, and he is ready to share the story. He has also established the narrator's position. He will now designate a physical area or "box" on his right for the conductor and another on his left for the violinist.*)

(b)   Over here . . . (*The actor points to his right and then steps into the imaginary box to which he has just pointed.*)

(c)   . . . is a conductor. (*The actor mimes conducting with appropriate gestures.*)

(d)   Over here . . . (*The actor points to the left of the narrator's box and moves into that position.*)

(e)   . . . is a violinist. (*The actor mimes playing the violin and then moves into the narrator's position in the center. The conductor's position has now been established as being to the right of center, the violinist's position as being to the left of center.*)

(f)   The conductor . . . (*Staying in the narrator's box, the actor points to the conductor's position.*)

(g)   . . . conducts. (*Still in the narrator's position, the actor mimes conducting.*)

(h)   The violinist . . . (*The actor stops conducting and points to the violinist's position.*)

(i)   . . . plays. (*Still in the narrator's position, the actor mimes playing the violin.*)

The actor can execute the remaining lines from the narrator's position, or he can move into each character's position as described below.

(j)   The conductor says . . . (*The actor points to the conductor's position as he did when he pantomimed "over here," then moves into that position, assumes a physical gesture that serves as an "emblem" for the conductor, and substitutes a gesture for the word "says." That is, the actor points to the position, moves into it, reestablishes the character, and pantomimes the dialogue.*)

(k) "Watch my rhythm." (*The actor pantomimes this as the conductor.*)

(l) The violinist replies . . . (*The actor points to the violinist's position, moves into it, assumes the physical emblem that he has established for the violinist, and substitutes a gesture for the word "replies."*)

(m) "You're conducting too fast." (*The actor pantomimes this as the violinist.*)

In this exercise each character has his own position or box. The narrator occupies the center position and decides where the other characters' positions will be. The narrator is the actor, playing himself, and his objective is to direct the audience's focus and to help them follow and enjoy the story. Breaking the reality of a scene with narration can strengthen the story because narration involves direct contact with the audience. The characters other than the narrator must have strong physical activities or gestures that define them. Once they are established, simpler physical emblems (for example, tapping a baton or holding a violin or a bow) can be used to reestablish them for the audience. These physical emblems are especially useful if the pantomime is expanded to include many characters.

Exercise 4. The actor narrates a simple story. As he tells the story and introduces the characters, other actors step into the positions of the characters and act out the story. For example, "There once was a fisherman." (An actor goes to the position that the narrator points to and portrays a fisherman.) "And a fish." (Another actor goes to the fish's position and becomes a fish.) "The fisherman said to the fish . . ." (The actor playing the fisherman improvises a conversation using pantomime.) "The fish replied . . ." (The fish pantomimes an answer.) The story evolves with the narrator controlling who will speak and when. He can also change the environment. For example, "Suddenly they found themselves at the bottom of the sea." Or, "Then they were flying through the air." Finally, the narrator can control character transformations. For example, "Then they saw a whale and a dolphin." (The actors become these new characters.)

Exercise 5. The actors line up and improvise a story, each continuing the story from where the preceding actor left off. (See Spolin's "Story Building" and "Story Telling" exercises.)

Exercise 6. At this point the actors must work on their ability to share control of a story so that this function does not reside solely with the narrator. They must also learn to work as an ensemble and to become sensitive to where and when to give and take focus and how to reinforce as a group what the audience should focus on. We used four of Spolin's exercises here: "Give and Take," "Camera," "Dubbing," and "Working with Gibberish."

Exercise 7. The actors should also practice changing environments and immediately becoming part of a new environment. For example, an actor starts a story by saying, "It was a windblown desert." The actors create the environment by becoming camels, cacti, the wind, and the blazing sun. When the environment is established, it is then changed by another actor who might say, "Then they were under the sea." The actors immediately portray fish, plants, and water. The actors should work to find a way to physicalize *every* aspect of an environment, including the challenging ones like fire and sound. (In portraying a squeaky gate, for instance, one actor might be the gate, another the squeak.)

Exercise 8. The last step is to improvise within the created environment. All the work of the previous exercises must coalesce. The actors must be sensitive to what is happening where, and they must be able to give focus to it and to contribute to the dynamics of the story. They must be able to sense when the action within one environment is fading and when a new environment should be established. Above all, they must be aware that their objective is to share a story with the audience.

In addition to practicing the physicalization of stories, another major part of our rehearsal process was animal characterization. We worked together as a group to find the movement or the sound that most vividly suggested a certain animal. Sharing the creative process in this way contributed to the camaraderie and the spirit of the production as a whole.

From Spolin's "Drawing Objects" exercise we derived an animal drawing game. The judge selected an animal and whispered the name of that animal to a representative from each of two teams. They raced to their teams and drew the animal. The first team to guess the name of the animal won the game. The point of this game was not to draw the animal in detail but to select the most prominent or suggestive characteristic of the animal (the trunk of an elephant, the humps of a camel). We then repeated the game, using only the sound of the animal. Once again, the goal was to suggest the animal rather than realistically to duplicate its sound. Finally, we repeated the game a third time, "drawing" the animal with our bodies rather than with pencil and paper.

We tried to develop the animal characterizations in great depth regardless of how little of our work might finally be shown in performance. We explored a day in the life of an animal: How does it wake up, see, hear, eat, meet other animals, hunt, and play? We also investigated the area of behavior where animal and human characteristics come together and how these two sets of characteristics balance and interrelate. (For example, how does a squirrel gathering nuts for the winter resemble a miser storing away his gold nuggets?)

Various other exercises also helped. In one exercise each actor adopted the identity of an animal and sang songs, incorporating the sound of the animal and its movements into the presentation of the song. The snake hissed his way through "Yes, We Have No Bananas," and the coyote howled "Home, Home on the Range" and then harshly rasped out a version of "K-K-K-K-Katie." Other animals performed speeches from Shakespeare (with the elephant magnificently trumpeting, "O! that this too too solid flesh would melt . . ."). We also played animal musical chairs: when the music stopped, the animal who was left out had to improvise and persuade another animal to get up and to let him sit down. Finally, we brought it all together with an Ed Sullivan variety show. Ed was a giraffe, introducing the various animals who performed their human acts with often hilarious results.

By the end of the summer the show was complete. We had created it together, almost as a family. It was time to give it to an audience. On a clear fall morning a converted Jefferson Lines bus sat in front of the Guthrie. "Fables Here and Then" was painted in bold black letters on the silver chrome on both sides. The actors were leaving to share their work with almost fifty thousand people. The director presented the cast with a football signed with the date and the names of all the homefolk who would miss them and who wished them more than well. Pictures were taken, bottles of champagne presented. More pictures. Kisses. Waves. It was extravagantly sentimental. And it was wonderful.

Almost three months later that bus returned — grimy, mud-covered, the dirt thick enough to obscure the lettering on both sides. But there was a patch where some silver shone through. At one of our stops an audience member had decided to write us a fan letter, using his finger as a pen and the dirty bus as his paper. The anonymous graffito read, "Fables Company, We Love You."

David Feldshuh

Fables Here and Then

Characters

Six actors (four men and two women)

List of Fables

Act I

Act II

Assignment of Roles in *Fables Here and Then*

STORY	ACTOR I	ACTOR II	ACTOR III
The Wise Man	Neighbor/Bull/Rooster	Wise man/Rooster	Duck/Follower
The Centipede	Frog	Lizard	Owl
How the Snake Lost His Voice	Monkey	Snake	Cricket
Gassir the Hero	Blacksmith/Warrior	Warrior	Elder/Warrior
The Silver Bell	Jiro	Student	Old monk
The Shirt Collar	Iron/Clothing/Rag/Factory machine	Shirt collar	Bootjack/Rag/Clothing
The Suicide	Jury	Jury	Day
The Fisherman and the Sea King's Daughter	Urashima	Fisherman/Villager/Octopus	Fisherman/Villager/Crab/Eel
The Gas Company	Second gas man/Stove	Stove	First gas man/Stove
The Indians and Death	Indian	Indian/Old One	Indian
The Bremen Town Musicians	Farmer/Robber	Donkey	Cat

ACTOR IV	ACTOR V	ACTOR VI	STORY
Lazy man/ Follower	Wife/Follower	Neighbor/Pot/ Rooster/Follower	*The Wise Man*
Goose	Centipede	Crow	*The Centipede*
Lion	Pterodactyl	Earthworm	*How the Snake Lost His Voice*
Gassir	Partridge/Warrior	Warrior	*Gassir the Hero*
Mr. Mohei	Taro	Student	*The Silver Bell*
Clothing/Rag/ Washtub	Scissors/ Hairbrush/ Clothing/Rag	Girdle/Clothing/ Rag	*The Shirt Collar*
Jury	Neighbor	Wife	*The Suicide*
Monk/Fisherman/ Villager/Shark	Turtle/Fisherman/ Villager	Sea princess/ Fisherman/ Villager	*The Fisherman and the Sea King's Daughter*
Third gas man/ Stove	Fourth gas man/ Stove	English lady	*The Gas Company*
Great Shaman	Coyote	Indian	*The Indians and Death*
Dog	Rooster	Mouse/Robber	*The Bremen Town Musicians*

Act I

Director's Notes on *The Wise Man* (Chinese)

There is always someone who thinks he knows everything, and there are always people ready to believe him. This story is about such a person and the people who idolize him. Because "wise men" can exist only where the unwise abound, all the actors must help create the central character. They ravenously devour any crumbs of wisdom the wise man condescends to drop and display an ignorance equal to his pretension. His pretension becomes significant only insofar as it is greeted with devout respect. After some experimenting, we put this story first, using it to introduce the audience to the conventions of story theater. Its light satiric tone and its topical relevance enable it to serve as a gentle prologue to the stories that follow.

Three games were especially helpful in developing this story for the stage. The simple children's "telephone" game, in which a statement is whispered from one person to another and then the end product is compared with the original statement, was used to explore how the wise man's reputation was spread and maintained. This image of people passing along a statement ("that girl is fat") or emotion (crying at dinner) was the primary theatrical metaphor of the story.

The second and third games were taken from Spolin's *Improvisation for the Theater.* In the second game we improvised selling, buying, bargaining, lecturing, demonstrating, and storytelling using gibberish. This game was directly applicable to the market scene and to the scene in which the raging bull terrifies the town. The third game was the animal-drawing game described in the "Comments" section.

The Wise Man

Music. The actors enter, zealously following the wise man, the town celebrity. They ask his advice, comment on his pronouncements, point him out to friends. When he peremptorily cuts off the music, they freeze in a worshipful tableau.

WISE MAN

Once upon a time in a small town there lived a man who kept telling people how wise he was, until they all came to believe everything he said. (*searching, with a gesture*) I lost my hat. (*As in the "telephone" game, his statements and gestures change as they are passed along.*)

ACTOR I

He said, "That girl is fat."

ACTOR II

He said, "She's a ton if she's a pound."

ACTOR III

That girl is a mound.

ACTOR IV

The world is round.

ACTOR V

The world is round?

WISE MAN

Exactly. And they all came to ask his advice. (*Music. All follow the wise man, doing the things that people do in the presence of a wise man.*)

ALL

How wise he is! He's amazing! What a wise saying! (*All freeze.
The music stops.*)

LAZY MAN

In the same village there lived a man . . .

WIFE

. . . and his wife . . .

LAZY MAN

. . . who were so lazy that they . . .

LAZY MAN and WIFE

(*yawning, falling asleep*) . . . overslept every morning. (*A
rooster crows.*)

ACTOR III

(*hoeing*) Other people had been up for hours . . .

ACTOR IV

(*digging*) . . . tilling the fields . . .

ACTOR V

(*sawing wood*) . . . before those two lazy people . . .

ALL

(*in unison*) . . . even rolled out of bed. Ugh. (*All freeze in a
work tableau. The lazy man and his wife snore. Then the wife
wakes up.*)

WIFE

One morning . . .

NEIGHBOR

. . . a neighbor said to the lazy woman, "Why don't you get a
rooster, my dear?"

WIFE

What's that?

NEIGHBOR

That's a bird that crows in the morning, and it's bound to make
you jump out of bed.

WIFE

Oh, thank you, neighbor, for your advice. And the lazy woman
told her husband. (*waking him up*) Husband, the neighbor says
that we should get ourselves a rooster.

LAZY MAN

What's that?

WIFE

That's a bird that crows in the morning. It should wake us up.

LAZY MAN

Good idea. Let's get one of those wonderful birds. So the two set off for a nearby town where there was a market. (*The actors create a market scene. All freeze as the music ends.*) But they had never seen a rooster before in their lives. (*Four actors become three roosters and a duck waiting to be sold. Each rooster crows as the lazy man and his wife, interested but not satisfied, inspect it. They walk past the duck. It quacks. They turn slowly, beaming. The decision is made. They walk the happy duck home, put him under their bed, and fall asleep.*) They took him home with them, put him under their bed, and went peacefully to sleep.

DUCK

Quack.

ACTOR IV

Morning came. (*The three roosters crow loudly. The duck quacks quietly. The lazy man and his wife snore. After a pause the disgruntled roosters combine with music to wake the couple up.*)

WIFE

When the two finally woke up late that afternoon . . .

LAZY MAN

. . . they agreed that all was not in order with their rooster.

WIFE

It didn't crow this morning.

LAZY MAN

Well, what should we do?

WIFE

I'll take its temperature.

LAZY MAN

I think we better call the wise man.

WIFE

Good idea!

LAZY MAN and WIFE

Wise man! (*Music. The wise man strolls over with his entourage, spouting wise sayings such as "An apple a day . . . " and "A stitch in time . . . " His signal cuts off the music.*)

WISE MAN

What seems to be the problem?

WIFE

Well, we don't know, but he just didn't crow this morning. (*The wise man closely examines the duck; his eyes light up; he whistles.*)

WISE MAN

There's your problem! You see, you've trodden on this rooster's beak and flattened it out. No wonder the poor bird can't crow. (*The duck quacks. All applaud and follow the wise man. All freeze.*)

BULL

Some time later, the lazy man's bull broke out of his shed and started running around the yard. (*Music. The bull charges wildly. Chaos. All freeze.*) He suddenly saw an earthen pot on the ground and wanted the grain inside. (*An actor becomes the pot. The bull gets his head caught in the pot.*)

WIFE

The bull's head is in the pot.

LAZY MAN

(*grabbing a leg*) I'll pull the tail.

WIFE

I'll pull the pot. (*They pull three times, then give up.*)

LAZY MAN and WIFE

Oh, wise man! (*Music. The wise man, still spouting wisdom, saunters over.*)

WISE MAN

(*after a quick survey*) Your problem is that you have a bull with his head in a pot. Now if you want to get the bull's head out of the pot, you must cut it off.

WIFE

What a wonderful idea!

WISE MAN

That's true.

LAZY MAN

How wise you are!

WISE MAN

Don't mention it.

LAZY MAN

So the lazy man took a knife and — swish — the bull was without
a head.

WIFE

(*pointing*) But the head is still stuck in the pot.

LAZY MAN and WIFE

Wise man!

WISE MAN

Bash it on the ground.

WIFE

Why didn't we think of that ourselves?

LAZY MAN

Why didn't we? (*They smash the pot.*) The pot smashed into a
hundred pieces and the bull's head rolled free.

LAZY MAN and WIFE

Wise man, we can hardly tell you how grateful we are.

WIFE

Won't you please come and have supper with us tonight?

WISE MAN

Why, sure. But like I always say, one man's meat is another man's
poison. (*Music. All line up at a table and eat. The wise man begins
to cry.*)

ALL

What on earth is the matter?

WISE MAN

Grief floods my heart at the thought of you people left to your
own devices when I am no longer alive. (*Music. The wise man
cries again. They all cry in turn. The music stops. All freeze in a
tearful tableau.*)

ACTOR V

But they need not have cried because the wise man never died. In fact, he is still with us to this very day. (*He mimes holding a microphone toward the wise man, who delivers some topical statement such as "No, actually, I have no thoughts about '76." Music. The wise man exits, eagerly followed by autograph seekers, reporters, cameramen, and true believers.*)

Director's Notes on *The Centipede* (Anonymous)

A burst of light. The howl of a jazz quartet. Blazing onto the stage comes the centipede with a hundred tap-dancing feet, the original Busby Berkeley of the forest. Magnetized by her dance, the other animals flock to the glade and happily join the celebration. They rejoice in the centipede's gift — her ability to dance and to make others want to dance. When the festivities are finished and the frog foolishly asks the centipede to dissect the spirit that ignites her dancing feet, she is overwhelmed by the mystery of her own creation and loses her ability to dance. But the end of the story must emphasize that the loss is not hers alone. As the animals shared in the joy, they must share in the sorrow. Innocence is gone. They too will never dance again.

In choosing the animals for this story, we tried to achieve a balance of sound and movement. The frog jumped and growled his "ribbit"; a goose leaped and honked (don't ask what a goose was doing in a forest); a hissing, tongue-darting lizard crawled along the ground using only his arms, his legs becoming a tail; an owl waddled about, his wings flapping at his sides, slightly resembling a penguin but with a distinctive "whoo" that made the species clear; and the centipede waved her fluid arms in contrast to the precision of her tap-dancing feet. On his entrance each animal was given a moment of focus to establish his characterization; the resulting sound and movement made the congregation appear much larger than it was.

The Centipede

Music. A burst of light. In high-stepping vaudeville tradition the centipede taps her way onstage. The music stops.

CENTIPEDE

Once there was a centipede. Nightly she would dance an amazing dance that all the animals in the forest came to watch. (*Music. The dance continues. Other animals enter and join in. They applaud the centipede as the dance ends.*)

FROG

One evening the frog said, "How on earth do you know which foot to put down when?" (*The centipede thinks, turns to the other animals for an answer, then speaks to the audience.*)

CENTIPEDE

And the centipede never danced again. (*The lights slowly fade with the animals sadly examining wings, paws, and any movable part to find the answer to the frog's question.*)

Director's Notes on *How the Snake Lost His Voice* (Japanese)

The world of this story is a primeval forest — thick, dense, sultry green, a Rousseau jungle inhabited by creatures still tasting the miracle of their own birth. As the snake sings his melancholy song and the jungle yawns awake, we see not just another morning but the first morning, the dawn of creation. The lion, the pterodactyl, the monkey, the earthworm, and the cricket are born; they move, see, and hear for the first time, discovering themselves and the world around them. Awed by the world's newness and splendor and caressed by the snake's velvet voice, they feast their eyes on the beauty around them.

The character and the movements of the cricket contrast sharply with the serenity of this world. With short, energetic hops he springs through the forest, the first cunning middleman, slick and self-seeking. After he introduces deception into the world of innocence, the jungle turns cold and dark, becoming a less temperate, less sympathetic place to live.

How the Snake Lost His Voice

Music. The lights slowly come up. The animals move through the jungle. They rest.

SNAKE
Long, long ago the world looked altogether different from the way it looks now. The grass grew as high as the sky and the trees hardly came up to your knees. In those days the snake had a

beautiful deep voice, but he had no eyes. He was very proud of his voice and practiced singing from morning till night, with the result that there was no finer singer in the land. And when the snake sang his melancholy songs, the trees made music and the sleeping animals awoke and came to the meadow to listen for hours on end and marvel at the beauty of the world. (*The snake sings.**)

> *Night was dark but moonlit to my ear,*
> *And morning's sounds are sunrise.*
> *The world is loud.*

(*The animals gather around the snake, attracted by his beautiful voice.*)

ANIMALS

(*happily looking at the world*) Ahhh!

SNAKE

(*sad because he cannot see*) Ahhh. (*music*) And so the snake slipped into the blackness of his cave, which was no blacker to the snake than the meadow at noon. Ssss . . . (*Music. The snake goes back to his cave.*)

EARTHWORM

One morning an earthworm passed by. Now the earthworm was as unhappy as the snake but for a different reason. The earthworm had large dark eyes and loved to look at the world. She wanted to tell everyone all about it. (*The earthworm tries to speak to the other animals but cannot.*) But the earthworm had no voice. She looked at the other animals and tried to talk as best she could. (*The earthworm pantomimes: I love the rain; I love the flowers; I love to see.*) But the other animals didn't understand the earthworm's silent talk and so they didn't pay any attention to her. (*The animals slowly leave the stage. Music. The cricket dances into position.*)

CRICKET

Moving into the woods that day was a clever and ambitious cricket. Being small, he could see the woeful sadness in the

*Music on page 212.

earthworm's eyes. (*The cricket speaks to the earthworm, who answers the cricket's questions in pantomime. The cricket kreaches.*) Nice day, eh? What's the matter? Oh . . . And the cricket realized that the earthworm couldn't speak. (*The snake sings his song.*) And then he heard the beautiful, sad song of the snake (*the cricket offers the snake his hand to shake; the snake gropes blindly for it*) and realized that the snake couldn't see. He had an idea. Hello, Mr. Snake. That's certainly a beautiful voice you have. You must be proud of such a voice.

SNAKE

What good is it? (*groping*) I spend my life in darkness, so I can't enjoy the enchantment of springtime — the sight of blossoming trees, the colorful flowers. (*The cricket hands him a flower.*) My voice doesn't help me see a thing.

CRICKET

Mr. Snake, I think I can help you. (*The snake bumps into a branch and feels his way under it.*)

SNAKE

How can anyone help me?

CRICKET

The grief in your beautiful voice cannot leave a person as sensitive as myself unmoved. If you are willing to make some sacrifices, I think I can solve your problem.

SNAKE

I would sacrifice anything to see the world through my own eyes.

CRICKET

Anything?

SNAKE

Anything. My scales, my fangs, my coils . . . just tell me.

CRICKET

What about your voice?

SNAKE

My voice! How would giving up my voice help me see?

CRICKET

I know an earthworm with eyes . . .

SNAKE

What sort of eyes?

CRICKET

Large eyes.

SNAKE

How large?

CRICKET

As large as your voice and as dark as your cave.

SNAKE

But why would she give them to me?

CRICKET

Each of us believes his own sorrow is greater than anyone else's. If I know this earthworm, I'll bet my crooked legs that she'd be more than willing to exchange her eyes for your voice. What do you say?

SNAKE

I wouldn't miss my voice at all if only I could see! Will the earthworm do it?

CRICKET

We shall inquire immediately. (*Music. The cricket and the earthworm converse, the earthworm answering in pantomime.*) In a moment the cricket was speaking to the earthworm. Oh, Earthworm! The sadness in your beautiful eyes has touched my heart. I have spent a great deal of time considering how I could help you. Now listen. I know it is your dearest wish to speak of the world you have seen and to communicate with your fellow creatures. Miss Worm, I have found you a voice. A voice! I suppose you would give up practically anything for a voice. Like your burrow? Or your tail? What about your eyes? Why not? You've seen the world far long enough. But to be able to speak! To sing! To tell the world what you have seen. It's easily done. Your eyes for a voice. And not just any voice, but the voice, the snake's voice! (*The snake sings. The cricket leads the earthworm to the snake.*) Then is it a deal, Miss Worm? But then the cricket added as casually as he could: Well, of course, Miss Worm, I should expect some reward for my troubles. Oh, not much, I assure you

— a trifle. I should love to try out the snake's voice myself for just a short while before I give it to you. You don't mind, do you? Good enough. It took just a matter of moments for the two sorrows to change hands. (*Music. The animals enter excitedly. The cricket carries the earthworm's eyes to the snake.*) Oh, Mr. Snake, here they are!

SNAKE

Give, give, give . . . (*The cricket gives the earthworm's eyes to the snake. The snake sees for the first time and euphorically greets the other animals.*)

CRICKET

Now your voice, if you please. (*The snake sings. The cricket pulls the voice out of the snake as if it were a long cord. The snake's voice gets lower and lower until he is left with just a hiss.*) Ah, Miss Worm, here it is, the most beautiful voice in the world. (*The cricket gives the earthworm a note, then takes it away.*) Then the cricket remembered the arrangement. Wait, Miss Worm. Of course you remember our agreement. I get to try out the voice first. Oh, but now surely you've been without a voice for such a long time, why should a short while more make any difference? (*The earthworm sadly agrees.*) So the cricket went off to swallow his new voice. (*The cricket eats various notes, finally swallowing all of them.*) After forcing and shoving and struggling hard, the snake's entire voice was in the tiny cricket body. And that night all the animals in the forest came to the meadow to hear the cricket's new voice. (*The cricket sings with his new voice. The other animals gather around him, attracted by the sound. Music. Winter comes. The animals hibernate, huddling together for protection from the cold.*) Time passed from early summer to winter when the winds blow cold. The cricket came to love his new voice and never did return to the waiting earthworm. (*The cricket kreaches. The earthworm reaches out blindly, trying to find him. The cricket tricks her by sounding his voice, then sidestepping when she gets near.*) And when the earthworm came out to find the cricket she couldn't even shout. (*The earthworm pantomimes: I want my voice.*) She could not even look reproachfully at the cricket, for she no longer had any eyes. Ever since that time, whenever the cricket strikes up his merry tune, the earthworm appears and follows the sound. Not that it does any good (*kreach*), for the earthworm waits in vain and in darkness for the cricket to hand over her voice. (*Kreach. The cricket tricks the earthworm once more and goes to sleep. The lights slowly fade, leaving the earthworm blindly searching for something she will never find.*)

Director's Notes on *Gassir the Hero* (African)

In this African folktale the aggressive forces of war and might contend with the eternal spirit of peace and music. This duel is established during the partridge's song. During the song Gassir's angular, warlike movements, underscored by timpani and cymbals, oppose the soft, lyrical motion of the partridge. She circles Gassir, weaving her haunting melody to the accompaniment of a flute and the gentle, rustling chords of a guitar. The outcome of this visual battle between curves and straight lines is revealed in the story's closing tableau when the partridge, her wings undulating, stands above a humbled Gassir.

To capture the spirit of war physically, we abstracted elements from two Japanese martial arts, karate and kendo (stick fighting). A kata (a sequence of karate moves) was performed at the very beginning of the story by all six actors and was accompanied by strong, vibrant music that included the sounds of African drums. This immediately established a world in which aggression and strength are primary values.

The basic form of the kata we used is shown in Masatoshi Nakayama's book *Karate Kata Heian 1* (Kodansha International, 1968). The kata was executed by the actors from the positions indicated in the accompanying diagram. The actors returned to the same positions after the battle scene.

X
Partridge

X   X
Son   Son

X   X
Elder   Blacksmith

X
Gassir

Elements of kendo were used to represent the frenzy and the agony of the battle between Gassir and his sons and their enemies. In our production the kendo fight was divided into four sections, the intricacy of the battle increasing with each section. As each son was killed, he froze in a position of pain, and the stick he used as a weapon became the instrument of his death. The frenetic movement of battle contrasted sharply with the silent, contorted death tableau that grew from it.

The repeat of the partridge's song at the end of the story is a chant of resurrection. As each actor begins to sing, he breaks from his death position until all, sticks raised triumphantly, proclaim in unison, "Gassir, great hero!" The next section is a retreat from this assertion of heroism. The sticks are slowly lowered and the actors kneel, bowed before the power of song. On the partridge's last line, "And leave only my song," she rises slowly and stands above Gassir, gently waving her wings. A phoenix rising from the ashes of battle, she is the conqueror.

Gassir the Hero

*A roll of timpani begins in the darkness. As the lights slowly come up,
a kata is performed. The kata and the music end.*

GASSIR

Long, long ago there lived a famous hero by the name of Gassir.
He had conquered all his foes and laid waste their villages. All
feared him and he believed his fame would last forever. (*Music.
The partridge, wings gently waving, circles Gassir, weaving her
song.*)

PARTRIDGE

Returning from battle one day, Gassir came upon a partridge.
She was moving through the grass and singing:*

> *No swords that tame*
> *The foe will be remembered.*
> *The lofty warrior's fame*
> *Will be forgotten.*
>
> *Gassir, great hero,*
> *None will know*
> *Your name or who you are—*
> *And who will care?*
>
> *For fame feeds on force*
> *And breeds sorrow.*
> *And memory's course*
> *Stops tomorrow.*
>
> *The fighter and the fight*
> *Disappear within the night*
> *Of time — and leave only my song,*
> *And leave only my song.*

*Music on pages 213 and 214.

(*As the song ends, the partridge returns to her position.*)

GASSIR

Gassir listened to the bird's song and, full of anger, went to the elder.

ELDER

The partridge is right. A hero's fame is like the grass. It is dry before the season is over. But a song lives on forever. (*The sustained last note of the partridge's song is cut off by the sound of a blow from the blacksmith's hammer on an anvil. Gassir speaks, then goes to the blacksmith.*)

GASSIR

Thereupon Gassir went to the blacksmith. (*hammer blow*) Build me a lute.

BLACKSMITH

I'll build you a lute, but will you know how to play it?

GASSIR

That's my worry, not yours.

BLACKSMITH

So the blacksmith made him a lute. (*The blacksmith strikes his anvil three times. On the third blow, the crash of cymbals and timpani is changed to the sound of a lute. The blacksmith mimes handing Gassir the lute. Gassir tries to play it. It falls silent.*)

GASSIR

But when Gassir tried to play it, it made no sound. Why is the lute silent? (*hammer blow*)

BLACKSMITH

I told you you wouldn't know how to play it. But that's your worry, not mine. (*hammer blow*)

GASSIR

Tell me, what should I do?

BLACKSMITH

Your lute is only a piece of wood. It doesn't know how to sing: it has no heart. It is you who must give it a heart. (*hammer blow*) Take it with you into battle. When the wood is damp with your sweat and your tears, when your worries become its worries and your fame its fame, then it will no longer be just a piece of wood

that I fashioned into a lute, but a part of you, of your life.
(*hammer blow*) Then it will speak. (*Three hammer blows. Music.
All but Gassir exit.*)

GASSIR

It was not long before Gassir again found himself at war with one
of his enemies. (*All reenter with sticks for the kendo fight and
form a half-circle around Gassir.*) Gathering his five sons about
him, he said to them: Today we shall go into battle. Our deeds
must never be forgotten. The glory of our swords must live on
forever. I, Gassir, and you, my sons, may die in battle, but we
shall live on in song, which is immortal. So saying, he went forth
with his five sons. (*Music. Battle. The first son is killed; he
remains frozen in the position of his death. As the other sons are
killed, they also hold their positions. The music and the battle
stop for each of the following speeches.*) For five days they fought
as befitted heroes. (*Music. The battle resumes. The second and
third sons are killed.*) The blows of Gassir's sword made the lute
tremble. The sweat from his brow seeped into its wood. (*Music.
Battle. The fourth son is killed.*) For five days they fought as
befitted heroes, and each day he sacrificed one of his sons in the
dance of battle. (*Music. Battle. The last son is killed. Death
tableau.*) On the fifth day — the day of victory, but also the day he
buried his fifth son — the great warrior knelt and for the first time
in his life shed tears of grief. All his heroism had been in vain. He
was now bereft and alone, and soon no one would know anything
of him or his deeds. (*A guitar plays. The kendo stick used by
Gassir as a weapon now becomes the lute.*) Suddenly he heard a
song, a song that seemed to come from his own heart. It was the
lute, brought to life not by his heroic deeds but by his tears. (*As
the actors sing, they come out of the tableau.*)

WOMEN

(*singing*)
>No swords that tame
>The foe will be remembered.

GASSIR

(*speaking over the song*) And the lute sang of Gassir and his sons and their bravery, and its song lives on to this day and shall live on forever.

MEN

(*singing*)

> No swords that tame
> The foe will be remembered.

WOMEN

(*singing*)

> The lofty warrior's fame
> Will be forgotten.

MEN

(*singing*)

> The lofty warrior's fame
> Will be forgotten.

ALL

(*chanting in unison*)

> Gassir, great hero . . .

MEN

(*singing*)

> For fame feeds on force
> And breeds sorrow.

WOMEN

(*singing*)

> And memory's course
> Stops tomorrow.

ALL

(*singing*)

> The fighter and the fight
> Disappear within the night
> Of time — and leave only my song . . .

PARTRIDGE

(*singing*)

> And leave only my song.

(*The lights fade with the partridge standing above a humbled Gassir.*)

Director's Notes on *The Silver Bell* (Japanese)

Almost all the *Fables* included dances or choreographed movement. We therefore chose the last line of *The Silver Bell*, "What would the world be like if we all just danced and danced?" to be the subtitle of our production. Our answer is that it would be a world of irrepressible laughter, friendship, and love.

The key to *The Silver Bell* is that the characters cannot help but laugh and dance; when they see the bell and hear its sound, they have no choice. In spite of the seriousness they try to maintain, they begin to smile and their feet start moving. The moments when glumness yields to laughter are the most theatrical in the story and the most difficult to capture. But if they are captured, when the old monk opens his arms as if to ask the audience, "Will you dance, too?" the actors will not be dancing alone. This tale speaks to the laughter in all of us and asks us to express through dance the job of being alive.

The dance itself was an easy two-step and a hop. We chose the simplest step possible so that the actors would be free to focus on the emotion of the moment and on making contact with each other.

It is important that the bell be strongly established. Each actor should touch it in the same way and the sound of the bell should be consistent. Every time a character is made to laugh and dance, he should focus on the bell in order to reinforce it as the source of his transformation.

The Silver Bell

Music. The lights come up. An old monk is alone on the stage. He mimes tapping a bell. Its ringing makes him smile.

MONK

In a little town by the sea in Japan lived a kind old monk whose house stood on high ground next to a temple. The house had a pretty veranda, and from its roof hung a small silver bell (*he taps the bell*) attached to a strip of parchment on which was written a beautifully lettered poem:

Life? A butterfly
On a swaying grass.
That's all, but exquisite. (*bell sound*)

As soon as the breeze struck the parchment, it would begin to sway and set the little bell tinkling merrily. (*bell sound*) The old monk loved sitting in the garden. He would sit there for hours, looking out to sea and listening with a contented smile on his face to the bell tinkling. (*bell sound*) Life? A butterfly. (*Music. Mr. Mohei, an unhappy apothecary, enters.*)

MR. MOHEI

In the same town lived Mr. Mohei, the apothecary. For some time now his steps had been dogged by misfortune. One day his heart felt so full of sorrow he didn't think he could bear it for a moment longer. So he decided to go up the long hill to the temple and ask the old monk's advice. (*He moves to the old monk; he stops when he hears the bell ring.*) But when he got there and saw the old monk sitting contentedly on his veranda (*bell sound*) and heard the merry tinkling of the bell, it seemed as if a weight had suddenly been lifted from his heart, and it occurred to him that life would be much better if he could sit on his own veranda and listen to the merry tinkling of the bell. So shyly he turned to the monk and said: Excuse me, but I should very much love to borrow that wonderful bell of yours — just for one day.

MONK

I will gladly lend you my bell, but you must promise to return it first thing tomorrow morning or I shall be the one who is feeling sad. (*He hands Mr. Mohei the bell.*)

MR. MOHEI

Thank you, thank you. I promise. (*He returns home.*) Now when Mr. Mohei got back to his own house he immediately tied the bell to his own veranda roof. And the strangest thing began to happen to his sadness. (*Mr. Mohei mimes tieing the bell. It begins to ring. Music. Mr. Mohei starts to laugh and dance. The music ends and Mr. Mohei freezes.*)

MONK

The next morning the old monk rose early, waiting eagerly for Mr. Mohei to bring back the bell. Time passed, and when by midday Mr. Mohei still had not returned, the old monk began to feel a bit uneasy. Finally he called one of his pupils, young Taro, to him. Taro! (*Taro enters and bows.*) Taro, please run down the hill to the house of Mr. Mohei, the apothecary. He borrowed my silver bell and promised to return it this morning. Please remind him that I am waiting.

TARO

(*miming running as he speaks*) Taro hurried down to the apothecary's house. As he approached the house, he heard the merry tinkling of the bell. He could not believe what he saw. (*Music. Mr. Mohei resumes his dance.*) Mr. Mohei, my master sent me for the bell. Mr. Mohei! (*He tries to question Mr. Mohei but is drawn into the dance. Both freeze as the music ends.*)

MONK

Another hour passed and then another and still Mr. Mohei did not return the bell. When young Taro failed to return from his errand, the old monk began to feel quite anxious. Finally he called his other pupil, young Jiro, to him. Jiro! (*Jiro enters and bows.*) Jiro, please run down the hill to the house of Mr. Mohei, the apothecary. He borrowed my silver bell and promised to return it this morning. Remind him that I am waiting, and if you see young Taro on the way, please tell him that his master is surprised at his dawdling.

JIRO

(*miming running as he speaks*) Jiro ran down the hill determined to get the bell back. He approached the apothecary's garden and heard the merry tinkling of the bell. (*Music. Taro and Mr. Mohei resume their dance.*) But as he went through the gate, he could

hardly believe his eyes. (*turning to the dancing figures*) Taro!
What are you doing? Mr. Mohei, my . . . (*He is drawn into the
dance. The three freeze as the music ends.*)

MONK

Another hour passed and then another until the sun sank low in
the western sky. The old monk stood on the path in front of the
temple, but there was no sign of Mr. Mohei or either of the two
young pupils. Bewildered and unhappy, he waited, and the
sadness in his heart weighed more heavily than any he had ever
known. Finally, he put on his sandals and shuffled down the hill
to the apothecary's house. (*Music. The dance resumes. The monk
tries to question Mr. Mohei and the pupils, but he too is drawn
into the dance. They freeze as the music ends. Then Actor I enters
and speaks to the audience.*)

ACTOR I

And how, you may ask, does this story continue? Well, in order to
know that, we should have to send someone else to Mr. Mohei's
house to find out what was happening. (*Music. The dance
resumes. Actor I is drawn into the dance. All freeze as the music
ends. Actor II enters and speaks to the audience.*)

ACTOR II

But if he were to hear the merry tinkling of the bell and see those
five happy people dancing round and round the garden, he would
be irresistibly drawn into their dance and would forget to bring
back any news. (*Music. The dance resumes.*) Mr. Mohei, Mr.
Mohei . . . (*Actor II is drawn into the dance. All freeze as the
music ends.*)

MONK

And if in the end we went there ourselves (*all turn and face the
audience as if asking the question*), we too might be caught in the
very same way. And what would the world be like if we all just
danced and danced? (*The old monk taps an imaginary bell.
Music. As they all dance off, the old monk taps the bell once more
and beckons to the audience to join the dance. Blackout.*)

Act II

Director's Notes on *The Shirt Collar*
(Hans Christian Andersen)

To suggest an ambiance of antique elegance inhabited by delicate, fragile miniatures, we created a Victorian music box for this piece and brought its porcelain figurines to life to tell the story. With Old World grace and propriety these fading portraits of a passing age present the tale of a lonely shirt collar's vain courtships and misadventures.

Because the characters in this story are inanimate objects, the director should strive to give them as much personality as possible. They include a tough little muscle-flexing bootjack, who walks to the accompaniment of a bass drum; a seductive, whisper-voiced hairbrush; a teasing, snappy girdle; a ballet-dancing scissors of Teutonic temperament with legs that snap shut with precision and finality; a pugnacious iron that chugs like a steam engine; and, of course, the quixotic shirt collar, who is forced to live his last moments in rose-colored memories of things that never happened.

At the end of the story these nostalgic figures, now old and tattered rags, are devoured by a factory machine, the implacable image of the future. They are processed into paper and another existence for a new, less graceful time.

176

The Shirt Collar

Music. As the lights come up, the actors are discovered in a music box tableau. The music box plays, then stops.

ACTOR 1
> Once there was a wonderful music box with little porcelain figurines on its top. It would turn ànd tell delicate stories to all who would listen to its music. (*As the music box plays, each actor steps out, introduces his character, and bows to the audience and then to the other characters.*)

GENTLEMAN
> Not long ago there was a fine gentleman whose entire worldly possessions consisted of . . .

BOOTJACK
> . . . a bootjack . . .

GENTLEMAN
> . . . and . . .

HAIRBRUSH
> . . . a hairbrush.

SHIRT COLLAR
> But he had the most beautiful shirt collar in the world.

GENTLEMAN
> And it is about this that we shall hear a story.

SHIRT COLLAR
> The shirt collar was getting old and he began to think about marrying, and it happened one day that he . . .

GARTER
> . . . and a garter . . .

SHIRT COLLAR
> . . . met in the washtub. (*An actor becomes the washtub. Other actors become clothes being tossed about as the washtub tips back and forth.*) Hello, said the shirt collar. Never before have I

177

seen anything so slim and delicate, so elegant and pretty. May I be permitted to ask your name?

GARTER

I shan't tell you, said the garter.

SHIRT COLLAR

Where is your place of abode?

GARTER

Please! (*The washtub tosses the clothes.*)

SHIRT COLLAR

Perhaps you are a girdle? An undergirdle? (*He pulls her arm; it snaps to her side.*) For I see that you are for use as well as for ornament, my pretty miss.

GARTER

You ought not to speak to me. (*She slaps the shirt collar.*) I'm sure I haven't given you any encouragement.

SHIRT COLLAR

When anyone is as beautiful as you are, is not that encouragement enough? (*The washtub tosses the shirt collar and the garter into a compromising position.*)

GARTER

Don't come so close. You seem to be a gentleman.

SHIRT COLLAR

So I am, and a very fine one, too. I possess a bootjack and a hairbrush.

GARTER

Don't come so close. I'm not accustomed to such treatment.

SHIRT COLLAR

What affectation. (*The washtub throws them into an embrace.*) But just then they were taken out of the washtub, starched, and hung in the sun to dry. (*The soggy, dripping clothes line up.*)

GENTLEMAN

Then they were laid on an ironing board. (*They lean back, still sopping.*)

IRON

And along came the glowing iron, who thought he was a steam engine. (*The whistling iron chugs past, ironing the clothes.*)

SHIRT COLLAR

Oh! I am becoming another man and my creases are coming out. (*The iron attacks the shirt collar; the other clothes retreat.*) Oh, you burned a hole! Arrg . . .

IRON

Rag! (*He exits.*)

SHIRT COLLAR

The shirt collar was rather frayed at the edge . . .

SCISSORS

. . . so the scissors came to cut off the threads. (*She dances.*)

SHIRT COLLAR

Oh, you must be a dancer. How high you can kick! That is the most beautiful thing I have ever seen. No man can imitate you.

SCISSORS

I know that.

SHIRT COLLAR

You ought to be a queen. My worldly possessions consist of a fine gentleman, a bootjack, and a hairbrush. If only I had a kingdom. (*The music and the dance stop.*)

SCISSORS

What? Is that a proposal?

SHIRT COLLAR

Yes, if you wish. (*She scissors over and snips off a piece of the shirt collar.*) Ouch, ouch! Well, I shall just have to propose to the hairbrush. It is really wonderful what fine hair you have, madam. Have you never thought of marrying?

HAIRBRUSH

Well, yes, I have. But I'm already engaged . . .

BOOTJACK

(*coming up behind the shirt collar*) . . . to the bootjack.

SHIRT COLLAR

Engaged?

BOOTJACK

Engaged.

SHIRT COLLAR

Oh. Now there was no one to marry, so he took to despising

matrimony. Time passed (*all the figures age to the sound of a ratchet*) and the shirt collar came in a ragbag to the paper mill. (*Factory whistle. Music. An actor becomes a machine; the other actors become rags.*) There was a large assortment of rags. Some fine ones . . .

FINE RAGS

Hello! (*They flop politely into a pile.*)

SHIRT COLLAR

. . . and some coarse ones.

COARSE RAGS

Hi! (*They flop roughly onto the fine rags.*)

SHIRT COLLAR

They all had much to tell. (*All speak at once, the shirt collar above the rest.*) But no one more than the shirt collar, for he was a hopeless braggart. I have had a terrible number of love affairs. They gave me no peace. I was such a fine gentleman, so stiff with starch. I had a bootjack and a hairbrush that I never used. You should have seen me then. Never shall I forget my first love. She was a girdle, so delicate and soft and pretty. She threw herself into the washtub for my sake. Then there was the dancer who inflicted the wound that has caused me to be here now. She was very violent. My own hairbrush was in love with me and lost all her hair in consequence. Yes, I have experienced much in that line. But I grieve most of all for that garter . . . I mean, the girdle . . . who threw herself into the washtub. I have much on my conscience. It is high time for me to become white paper. (*Factory-machine music. The machine processes the rags into crisp paper. After passing through the machine, the actors assume the original relationships of the music box tableau. With a gentle "shhhh" the stiffness melts away and the figurines of the music box reappear.*)

GENTLEMAN

And so he did. (*The music box gently plays out as the lights fade.*)

Director's Notes on *The Suicide* (Contemporary)

The Suicide is a modern fable, capturing absurdities indigenous to the twentieth century. Newspapers are well stocked with tales of this kind, and if the director wishes to give a contemporary touch to Act I, similar stories can easily be found, evolved, and added.

Such stories require a strong dramatic style that will structure them and give them a point of view. We produced *The Suicide* in what might be termed High Vaudevillian Crass — loud, brassy, and colorful. We recreated the most obvious vaudeville moves and visual tableaux and turned the story into a song-and-dance routine. It was executed in time with music, and the music controlled the rhythm of the actors' movements and of the story as a whole. By using the vaudeville world, a world in which falls are never fatal, the comedy of the story was heightened and its unpleasant aspects diminished.

The Suicide

Music. Lights. The actors dance into position. Day, his wife, and a neighbor testify before a jury of three.

DAY
   On trial in northwest Hungary was a man called Janus Day. (*Music. Dance: The wife comes forward.*)
WIFE
   Day was married to a nagging wife. (*Music. Dance: The wife nags Day.*)
DAY
   As he did not want to get rid of her, he spent a good deal of time

considering how she could be brought to her senses. (*Music. Dance: Day thinks.*) Finally, he evolved a plan in which fear and guilt would play important roles. (*Music. Dance: Day is struck with an idea.*) He would fake suicide. (*Music. Dance: Day demonstrates his idea.*)

WIFE

His wife left to go shopping. (*Music. Dance: The wife leaves.*)

DAY

While she was out, Day constructed a safety harness and climbed into it. Shortly before she was due back, he suspended himself, a convincing corpse, from the ceiling of their bedroom. (*Music. Day hangs himself. The music changes. The wife returns home.*)

WIFE

His wife returned and, seeing what she believed to be her dead husband, she screamed (*she screams*) and fainted. (*She faints. The neighbor comes forward.*)

NEIGHBOR

The woman next door heard the scream and hurried over to see what had happened. (*Music. Dance: The neighbor runs to Day and his wife, sees the "corpses," and gasps.*) Ahhh! She found what she thought were two corpses. (*Music. The neighbor starts to run away, then reconsiders.*) But not one to miss an opportunity, she decided to loot the apartment before she called the police. (*Music. She loots the apartment.*) As she was leaving the apartment with the loot (*she stops*) . . .

DAY

. . . the hanging corpse lifted its foot and gave her a good kick. (*Music. Day kicks her.*) She died of a heart attack. (*Music. The neighbor dies. Music. The jury dances, reaching its verdict. The dance ends.*)

JURY

Not guilty!

DAY

Day was acquitted on a charge of manslaughter. He told the court . . . (*Music. The wife comes forward.*)

WIFE

. . . that his wife's nagging had stopped. (*Musical finale. The actors form a beaming tableau, with Day hanged in the middle. Blackout.*)

Director's Notes on *The Fisherman and the Sea King's Daughter* (Japanese)

In *The Fisherman and the Sea King's Daughter,* as in the other stories in *Fables,* physical presentation must reinforce and add texture to the thematic content. In this story the illusion of floating in water is the fundamental physical motif. Almost all the action and the narration are cushioned by gentle undulations that suggest floating in a boat or underwater. This helps create a world of rounded edges and fluid motion, one where there is no firm ground to stand on. Because the pattern of movement visually suggests a world that is constantly changing, the feeling is conveyed that the supernatural events of the story are part of an even greater mystery, the mystery of the sea.

A superb film, useful in research for this story and a number of the other stories in *Fables,* is *A Night at the Peking Opera,* produced by Claude Jaeger in 1957. Copies of the film are available in many public libraries and from Film Images, 17 West 60th Street, New York, New York 10023.

The Fisherman and
the Sea King's Daughter

Music. Lights. The actors hum as they mime rowing boats out to sea and casting nets. As the song ends the fishermen exit, pulling in their catches. Urashima throws out his net once more. The motion of the water beneath him is continuous.

URASHIMA

In a small village by the sea lived a young fisherman called Urashima, who lived with his aged parents whom he loved very much. Every day he rose at dawn to take his boat out with the other fishermen. But then he would go on alone to the deepest parts of the sea and cast his nets in search of food. One day as he was waiting for his nets to fill, a huge wave washed under his boat. (*wave*) And to his amazement, struggling in his net was the most beautiful fish he had ever seen, shimmering with all the colors of the rainbow. (*The sea princess enters. She struggles to escape Urashima's net.*) The fish seemed to cry out . . .

SEA PRINCESS

Let me go! Let me go!

URASHIMA

. . . and the fisherman took pity on it: Go on. Go back to your home in the sea. (*He lets her go.*) The next day when the fisherman returned to the same spot . . .

TURTLE

(*singing offstage*) Urashima . . .

URASHIMA

. . . he heard the sea echo his name.

TURTLE

(*entering and singing*) Urashima . . .

URASHIMA

He turned and saw . . .

TURTLE

    . . . a bright green turtle that stretched out its head and spoke in a human voice: Urashima, I have been sent to you by the King of the Seven Seas, who lives in the Dragon Palace beneath the ocean. (*wave*) Yesterday you saved his daughter's life, and in return he invites you to his palace, where no human being has ever been. Follow me and I will take you there. (*Urashima hesitates.*) Don't be afraid. The ocean is my friend. It will let us pass. (*He sings: Urashima.*)

URASHIMA

    Urashima wanted very much to see the Dragon Palace, which no human being had ever seen before. (*The singing continues: Urashima.*) And as he did not wish to keep a king waiting, he jumped from his boat and followed the turtle to the bottom of the sea. (*Both jump into the sea and journey to the bottom. Sea creatures enter.*) When they reached the sea bed, Urashima saw before him all the animals and plants of the sea kingdom and a magnificent palace of red coral and mother-of-pearl set on pillars of blue light. (*The sea princess, in the form of a silver fish, swims past.*) A silver fish swam past him. As he followed it, it suddenly turned into the most beautiful woman he had ever seen. (*The fish changes into the sea princess. Other sea creatures swim around Urashima and the sea princess.*)

SEA PRINCESS

    I am the Princess of the Dragon Palace, and I owe you my life. Today all the inhabitants of my father's kingdom have been summoned to banquet and dance in your honor. I hope you will like your life at the palace. (*music*)

URASHIMA

    Suddenly a long fanfare of seashells sounded and the sea began to dance. (*The sea creatures dance around Urashima.*) The turtles swayed, the eels writhed and twisted this way and that, the shark and the octopus danced together, the crab stepped sideways, and the flying fish executed great leaps in time to the music and waved his fins like flowing veils. But suddenly the fisherman became frightened. (*The dance ends.*)

SEA PRINCESS

I am sorry that you want to leave us, Urashima. I was hoping that you would stay with us forever. I am sure you would get used to living in the palace, for you would be among friends and enjoy a position of honor. Won't you think it over? You may not like your life on earth so much after living with us here.

URASHIMA

Thank you, but I yearn to see my parents and spend my days out in the fresh air.

SEA PRINCESS

Please stay.

URASHIMA

Forgive me.

SEA PRINCESS

Go then, if you must. But before you go I want to give you something. Take this little box. (*She mimes throwing a box to him; he catches it.*) It contains a magic sea stone, the most precious substance in all the world. Urashima, you must never open the box. Just whisper to it and it will fulfill your every wish. But remember, you must never open it. Good-bye, Urashima. I fear for your happiness. (*Music. Sea journey back to the surface. The sea creatures swirl around Urashima and exit. The lights change. Urashima somersaults onto the beach. The music ends abruptly.*)

URASHIMA

Suddenly the fisherman found himself alone on a white beach as if it had all been a dream. And though everything seemed familiar, yet it all looked different somehow. (*He calls.*) Yo-o-o-o! (*He is answered by an echo.*) He recognized the bay and the headland, but where his cottage should have been there was only a stretch of sand, and the pine grove was much thicker and larger than before. (*He calls again.*) Yo-o-o-o! When he went to the village to inquire after his parents, no one seemed to know him or to pay any attention to him. (*Villagers enter, working: washing clothes, carrying water, sawing wood.*) Hello. Isn't this Sushima? My name is Urashima. Do you know my parents? What happened to the cottage on the beach? My name is Urashima. Do you know me? What happened to the cottage on the beach? Where are my parents? (*The villagers freeze in work positions, becoming cemetery statues.*) In an old cemetery outside the village all his questions were answered. For there on a single gravestone were the names of his parents, and the date was almost exactly the day he had left to see the Dragon Palace. (*He cries in anguish.*) Yo-o-o-o! (*A monk enters, blessing the stones of the cemetery.*)

MONK

When he saw a monk passing nearby, he turned to him for help.

URASHIMA

My name is Urashima. Do you know me?

MONK

No. I have never met you, have I?

URASHIMA

But I am a native of this village.

MONK

I'm sorry. I know no one named Urashima and I have lived here some fifty years . . . Urashima . . . yes, I think I remember now. An old legend I once studied about a young man who went to sea when it was perfectly calm and was never found again. All they found was his boat, anchored in the bay. But that could not have been you, young man. That was some three hundred years ago. (*Music. The statues becomes fishermen in their boats, slowly rowing out to sea. They hum the melody of the first song.*)

URASHIMA

All at once Urashima realized what had happened. It became clear to him that in the palace under the sea time passed much, much more slowly than on earth and that the few moments spent in the Dragon Palace represented three whole centuries in the world he had left behind . . . and that his parents and the people and the places he had known were now but the faintest echoes of memory. It must be a dream, he thought, until he looked into his hand and saw the magic box. He remembered the Princess's warning, waited a moment, and then opened it. (*He opens the box. During the next lines he ages and dies.*) His hand became gnarled. His back bent. He rushed to the brook and in it saw the shriveled face of an old, old man — turning quickly to dust. (*As Urashima opens his mouth to cry out, the sound is made by a fisherman, sighting something and pointing.*)

FISHERMAN

Yo-o-o-o! (*Urashima slumps to the stage. A wave passes under the boats.*) Look, out in the bay, the shadow of a man riding a giant turtle, and a beautiful silver fish leaping and swimming alongside! (*wave*)

URASHIMA

Perhaps what the fisherman thought he saw was the spirit of Urashima, returning to live forever with the Sea King's daughter in the Dragon Palace beneath the sea. (*The fishermen cast their nets, one after another. The lights slowly fade as the music ends.*)

Director's Notes on *The Gas Company*
(Contemporary)

The Gas Company was one of our most popular stories, a modern fable about man's inability to cope with a mechanical age and computerized organization. The theatrical metaphor of the story was a carnival carousel. The English lady stands at the center of the stage with the stove next to her, and the other actors circle, one by one, telling the story to the audience.

For the humor of the story to work the actors must play for clarity and let the confusion take care of itself. Each statement must be made as precise as possible. It is the sequence of statements and the momentum of the sequence that must overwhelm the audience. To make each statement totally explicit we underlined every vital statistic with a gesture. The days of the month, the number of gas men, and the actions ("investigated, thanked her, and left," "connected," "disconnected,") all were clarified by appropriate gestures. Each stove had a flame and the number of fingers used to mime the flame told the audience the number of the stove.

It is important that the audience not suspect too soon that they cannot keep up with the momentum of the story. They must be allowed to discover only as the story progresses that the physical movement is evolving into a carousel. At the beginning of the story, therefore, everything should appear completely normal, and any hints of carousel movement should be underplayed.

Pace is obviously crucial in achieving both these goals. It should be leisurely in the beginning, as if the first phone call will solve the problem. Music is also important. In our production it began as single, disparate notes. As the pace of the story increased, the frequency of these notes also increased, finally filling in and becoming carousel music. The result was that the carousel metaphor gradually unfolded both visually and musically.

The Gas Company

Music. Lights. A gas stove sits near the English lady. Other actors, in line, suggest the rise and fall of carousel horses.

ENGLISH LADY

On the first of May, 1962, the weather was overcast with a bit of rain in the northern districts, and the gas oven (*the stove hisses*) owned by a retired schoolmistress living at Glenfield in the county of Leicestershire developed a leak. (*hiss*)

GAS MAN 1

(*circling*) The gas company said they would send a man to investigate.

ENGLISH LADY

On the second of May there was no change in the weather.

GAS MAN I

A man arrived. He investigated, thanked her, and left.

ENGLISH LADY

On the third of May . . .

GAS MAN II

. . . two men arrived, removed her oven (*hiss*) . . .

GAS MAN III

. . . connected a second, smaller oven (*hiss*), and departed with the first. (*Hiss. They put the second oven in the place of the first.*)

ENGLISH LADY

On the fourth of May . . .

GAS MAN II

. . . two men delivered a third, extra oven. (*hiss*)

ENGLISH LADY

As there was no room in the kitchen . . .

GAS MAN III

. . . they left it in the garden. (*Hiss. They leave the third oven near the second oven.*)

ENGLISH LADY

On the fifth of May . . .

GAS MAN IV

. . . a man called, investigated, and left.

ENGLISH LADY

The sixth was a Sunday. (*A man steps forward to knock.*) Nobody called. (*He stops, then returns to the carousel line.*) On the morning of Monday the seventh . . .

GAS MAN II

. . . a man called and said: There has been a mistake.

ENGLISH LADY

That afternoon . . .

GAS MAN III

. . . two men called. They investigated, thanked her, and left.

ENGLISH LADY

On the eighth of May . . .

GAS MAN II

  . . . two men called, carrying the original, leaky oven. (*hiss*)

ENGLISH LADY

  As there was no room in the kitchen . . .

GAS MAN III

  . . . they left it in the garden beside the third oven. (*hiss*)

GAS MAN II

  We have no instructions to connect or remove anything. (*The stoves hiss three times in unison.*)

ENGLISH LADY

  The presence of the three ovens worried the retired schoolmistress. She telephoned the gas company. (*She mimes telephoning.*)

GAS MAN II

  Nobody called for seven days.

ENGLISH LADY

  On the fifteenth of May the weather was fair.

GAS MAN III

  Two men arrived from the gas company. They disconnected the second, smaller oven (*hiss*) . . .

GAS MAN II

  . . . carried the third, extra oven in from the garden (*hiss*), connected it, and departed . . .

GAS MAN III

  . . . with the second oven (*hiss*), leaving the original, leaky oven in the garden. (*hiss*)

ENGLISH LADY

  On the morning of May the twenty-first . . .

GAS MAN II

  . . . two men arrived to collect the third, extra oven. (*hiss*)

GAS MAN III

  Observing that it was already connected, they left, saying: We have no authority to disconnect.

ENGLISH LADY

  During the afternoon of the twenty-first . . .

GAS MAN I

   . . . a man arrived and disconnected the third, extra oven (*hiss*) and connected the original, leaky oven. (*hiss*)

GAS MAN III

   It was still defective. (*hiss*)

GAS MAN II

   He left the third, extra oven in the garden. (*hiss*)

ENGLISH LADY

   On the twenty-eighth of May . . .

GAS MAN I

   . . . two men collected the third, extra oven from the garden. (*hiss*)

ENGLISH LADY

   On the thirtieth of May . . .

GAS MAN III

   . . . a man called to see if everything was in order.

ENGLISH LADY

   On June the fifteenth . . . (*By now the actors all are circling, forming a carousel.*)

GAS MAN II

   . . . a man called and apologized for the other nineteen men. (*The carousel speeds up. The English lady surrenders. Blackout.*)

Director's Notes on *The Indians and Death* (American Indian)

The Indians and Death was staged as a religious ceremony, a ritual reenactment of Death's entrance into the world. The story has mythic dimensions, and to help achieve this on the stage we juxtaposed improvised movement and ceremonial movement.

The improvised movement took the form of a diffuse and unpredictable "tag" game. As the story progresses the game takes on more profound overtones: the Indians viciously "tag" food from one another during a time of famine; the coyote "tags" each member of the tribe with his idea to bring Death into the world; and, finally, Death "tags" and takes life.

Other movement in the story was structured and ceremonial; this included the rituals of going to the Sacred Rock, shooting the arrows into the sky, and making the decision to bring Death into the world. These and other rituals were enacted with precise, defined, and controlled movement. It should appear that they have become formalized through custom and years of repetition.

American Indian art, particularly masks, totems, and sand painting, was very helpful in suggesting images for this story.

The Indians and Death

Music. The lights slowly come up. The Indians and the coyote happily play "tag." The Great Shaman watches them, then turns to the audience.

GREAT SHAMAN

Long, long ago neither the Indians nor the animals were subject to Death. They all lived forever, and there were still food and room enough for everyone. (*The coyote howls. The game continues. The coyote goes to each Indian, trying to convince him.*)

COYOTE

Only the coyote complained: Why do we have to be squashed here like this? If only the old were to die, we'd be much better off. Let's bring Death into the world. Let's bring Death into the world. But he was ignored by everyone, until winter came (*it turns cold; the game becomes searching and fighting for food*) and the lakes froze and the food disappeared. (*The coyote goes from one Indian to another.*) There, you see? I told you. There are too many of us and that's why we're hungry. If only the old were to die, there would be plenty to eat for all of us. (*He wrests food from the Old One. All the Indians are cold and hungry.*)

GREAT SHAMAN

(*walking among them*) The Great Shaman of the tribe walked among his people, saw their hunger, and finally called them together at the Sacred Rock. (*Music. The Indians, humming, follow the Great Shaman to the Sacred Rock.*) As the firelight shadows danced, the Great Shaman spoke against the coyote's idea of bringing Death into the world.

COYOTE

(*howling*) But the coyote said: Oh, Great Shaman, I never intended to harm anyone. It's just that we cannot all survive. I simply suggest that we make a hole in heaven (*pointing*) and the dead can move up there — for a time. Then when there is again enough food for all, we will simply call them back. (*The coyote howls. The Great Shaman turns to his people, asking for their decision. Each Indian steps forward in turn and bows his head in assent. Music. All mime preparing their bows to shoot arrows into the sky.*)

GREAT SHAMAN

Daylight came and the best marksmen assembled . . .

COYOTE

Let us bring Death into the world.

GREAT SHAMAN

. . . to build a ladder to the sky.

COYOTE

Let us bring Death into the world. (*The Indians line up; they fit arrows to their bows.*)

GREAT SHAMAN

The plan was to shoot an arrow that would pierce the clouds (*the first arrow is released*), and then the second into the first (*second arrow*), a third into the second (*third arrow*), a fourth (*fourth arrow*), fifth (*fifth arrow*), sixth (*sixth arrow*), and so on (*the series continues, then finishes*) until a great ladder between heaven and earth would be formed. The Great Shaman saw that it was strong and said to his people: Death will now come into the world. (*The coyote howls. The Indians and the coyote happily resume their "tag" game.*) The Indians and the animals were pleased with their work and hoped for a better future. Although they knew their loved ones would leave them for a while, they knew they could someday return. (*The coyote howls, then "tags" the Old One, who goes onto his knees, crosses his arms, and bows his head as if dead. The "tag" game ends. The Indians stand with their dead as if before the Sacred Rock.*)

COYOTE

After the first Indians had died, the coyote's plans became more definite. He sharpened his teeth until they could cut his own tongue, and in the last hour before evening, when everything was absolutely still, he crept stealthily to the ladder in front of the Sacred Rock. (*The coyote travels to the Sacred Rock. The Great Shaman narrates as the coyote mimes the story.*)

GREAT SHAMAN

He stopped at the foot of the cliff and listened. All was silence except for the whistling of the night wind. Standing on his hind legs, he seized hold of the last arrow with his teeth and began to gnaw at it. The soft wood gave way, but the ladder stood fast. In a rage, the coyote shook the line of arrows, hoping to pry the first one loose. He succeeded only too well, and with a resounding crash the line of arrows came tumbling down and the dead disappeared forever. (*The Indians reach up to heaven, asking for the return of the dead. The Great Shaman turns to the Indians.*) It is done. They cannot hear us calling. The dead can never again return to the land of the living. (*The coyote howls. The Great Shaman speaks to the coyote.*) We have too long been patient with you. You must leave our midst as punishment. Go out into the prairie, where you will henceforth dwell alone and do no more evil. (*The coyote runs away from the Great Shaman and continues running until the end of the story.*) Go to sleep now, but from this day on Death will always be with us. (*The coyote howls. The Indians play "tag," trying to escape from an imaginary person, Death. As the Great Shaman narrates each death, that actor freezes in the position of the animal or the person he portrays.*) Night settled over the land, the night in which Death walked free in Indian country — the night in which the old badger died in his den (*first death*), the lonely hunter in his cabin (*second death*), the eagles in their eyrie high among the rocks (*third and fourth deaths; the coyote howls and frantically tries to escape his own death*). And although the coyote's pleas are often heard, there is no pity for him. Nor is he allowed to return to the land of the living, just as Death, whom he so callously brought into the world, can never again return to its abode high above the Sacred Rock. (*The Great Shaman turns to the coyote and points. The coyote howls and dies as the light fades.*)

Director's Notes on *The Bremen Town Musicians* (Jacob and Wilhelm Grimm)

The Bremen Town Musicians is a story of an impossible dream, of four discarded but deeply lovable animals triumphantly rejuvenated by their hopes for the future. When the donkey confides, "We're going to Bremen to become the town musicians," he is sharing the most important dream of his life, the source of his pride and hope. The dream must be treated with great respect for the story to work.

Once we had established the animals, the simplest emblems served to maintain their identity: the donkey brayed and had hands like hooves; the cat meowed and showed his claws; the dog panted, tongue hanging, and scratched and patted himself; and the rooster crowed and strutted as best he could. The movements of all the animals, though slowed by the realities of their age, were spurred on by a buoyant and heady optimism.

The fight at the end of the production was performed as if in total darkness. (Here, as in *The Fisherman and the Sea King's Daughter,* the film *A Night at the Peking Opera* was a helpful resource.) The animals encounter each other and the robbers by mistake, and misplaced bites, kicks, and scratches all add to the chaos. When the fight is over, the animals tentatively search for each other, quietly braying, barking, meowing, and crowing the opening lines of the finale song. As they realize that they are safe, all joyously break into song and dance as the lights come up.

The Bremen Town Musicians

Music. Lights. A farmer and a donkey enter. The farmer whips the donkey, who falls to his knees.

DONKEY

Hee-haw. Once there was a donkey. For years he had carried sacks of corn to the mill, but he was getting older and older and his strength was ebbing. (*The farmer whips the donkey.*) Hee-haw.

FARMER

One day the donkey's master looked at the donkey and said: This donkey is too old to earn its keep. I will cut off his head and send him to the glue factory. (*hee-haw*) And the farmer went for an ax. (*The farmer exits.*)

DONKEY

(*crying*) Hee-haw. Hee-haw. (*He hears in his bray a sound that impresses him. He brays again.*) Hee-haw. Suddenly the donkey had an idea: I'll go to the city of Bremen. There, he said to himself, I will surely become the town musician. Hee-haw. (*Music. The donkey travels toward Bremen. A dog enters, barking, and chases the donkey. The donkey stops him.*)

DOG

Are you a pheasant?

DONKEY

No. (*The dog barks and chases the donkey again. They stop, tired.*)

DOG

Some sort of fowl?

DONKEY

(*kicking his hind legs*) I'm a donkey. Hee-haw. See? (*The dog collapses and cries.*) What's the matter?

DOG

Oh, I used to be a hunting dog (*he howls and shows off his hunting point*), but now I'm getting too old to get the birds for my master. If I don't get a pheasant this time, he will shoot me for sure. (*The dog cries. The donkey thinks he hears musical potential.*)

DONKEY

Listen, can you sing?

DOG

I can bark. (*The donkey trots away, unimpressed.*) I can howl. (*The donkey listens, then harmonizes.*)

DONKEY

Listen, I'm going to Bremen to become the town musician. Would you like to come along?

DOG

It's better than getting shot.

DONKEY

It's better than being sent to the glue factory, too. Hee-haw. (*The dog barks. Music. They travel toward Bremen. Suddenly a mouse enters, chased by a cat. The mouse outruns the cat.*)

CAT

Meow. Aw, nuts. (*The dog investigates and discovers the cat. A fight breaks out; the donkey separates them. The cat starts to cry.*)

DONKEY

Mr. Cat? What's wrong?

CAT

Oh, I'm just getting too old to catch the mice. Now my mistress wants to poison me and make a fur cap out of my hide. Meow, meow. (*The cat cries. The donkey listens, impressed.*)

DONKEY

Mr. Cat, can you sing?

CAT

Can I sing! Listen to this. (*The cat meows the musical phrase that corresponds to the words "but we'll travel along" from the finale song "Side by Side." The first two times he fails to reach the last note.*)

DONKEY

Take your time. (*The third time the cat is successful, and the donkey and the dog harmonize their bray and bark on the notes corresponding to the words "singing a song." All are very pleased.*) Listen, we're going to Bremen to become the town musicians. Would you like to join us?

CAT

Meow!

DONKEY

Hee-haw!

DOG

Bark! (*Music. The three travel. A rooster enters; he tries to crow but fails.*)

ROOSTER

Cock-a-doodle-doo. (*He coughs and tries again.*) Cock-a-doodle-doo. (*He spits and tries again.*) Cock-a-doodle-doo. (*He whines.*) Eehh.

CAT

(*imitating*) Cock-a-doodle-doo . . . eehh.

DONKEY

What kind of rooster goes "Cock-a-doodle-doo . . . eehh"?

ROOSTER

An old one. I can't crow any more. When I crow at sunrise, everyone thinks they're just having nightmares and they roll over and go back to sleep. Age is cruel, my friend. (*He squawks, darts away, then stops to explain.*) And now the farmer is looking for me with an ax to chop my head off and make me into rooster soup. (*He crows.*)

DONKEY

Could I hear that crow again? (*speaking to the others*) You give a listen, tell me what you think. (*They "audition" the rooster. After false starts, they harmonize — braying, barking, meowing, and crowing — the notes corresponding to the words "it doesn't matter at all."*) It's not much of a crow, but it's a great soprano.

ROOSTER

A great soprano?

DONKEY

Listen, we're going to Bremen to become the town musicians. Would you like to come along? (*The rooster crows, the dog barks, the cat meows, and the donkey brays. Music. The four travel. The music slows as they grow tired and collapse.*) Halfway to Bremen night fell (*at the sound of a bass drum, night falls instantly; the donkey looks up*) and the animals tried unsuccessfully to sleep. (*Each goes to sleep in his own way.*)

ROOSTER

The rooster, who had flown up to the tallest tree to get some sleep, spotted a house in the distance. (*The rooster crows. All the animals think they are having a nightmare, roll over, and go back to sleep. The rooster wakes them.*) Wake up! Wake up! There's a warm, cozy-looking house just a short distance from here. I'm sure we'll be much more comfortable there. Besides, if we're going to be singers, we better be careful not to catch cold.

DONKEY

(*sneezing*) So the animals made their way to the place where the light was. (*Some robbers enter, laughing.*) Robbers! (*The animals, frightened, push the donkey to the window.*) So the donkey, being the biggest, had to go and look in the window. They have money! And they're feasting at a table full of food and drink!

ROOSTER

Is there any corn?

DOG

How I wish we were in there.

CAT

We have to figure out a way to drive them out. (*The animals converse.*)

DOG

So the dog, who was wise in the ways of men, said: We ought to attack them.

ROOSTER

They thought of a plan. At a given signal they would perform their music together. (*Each animal comes forward to demonstrate.*)

DONKEY

The donkey would bray. (*He brays loudly.*)

ALL

Shhh!

DOG

The dog would howl. (*He howls.*)

ROOSTER

The cock would crow. (*He crows.*)

CAT

And the cat would meow. (*He meows.*)

DONKEY

Then they would burst through the window and make a horrible noise.

CAT

The cat would spit and scratch like a witch. (*Hissing, he freezes in a ferocious position.*)

DONKEY

The donkey would kick like a monster with a wooden club. (*Braying, he joins the cat.*)

DOG

The dog would bite like a man with a knife. (*Barking, he joins the cat and the donkey.*)

ROOSTER

And the cock would crow as if it were the last judgment: This is all for you! Cock-a-doodle-doo! (*He completes the tableau.*)

ALL

Shhh! (*Music. They cautiously move to the window and form a pyramid.*)

DONKEY

So the donkey placed himself below the window.

DOG

And the dog climbed upon the donkey's back.

ROOSTER

And the cock climbed upon the dog's shoulders.

CAT

And the cat climbed upon the cock's shoulders.

DONKEY

And they waited for the robbers to put out the candle. (*The pyramid of animals leans and almost falls. A robber mimes blowing out the candle. The lights dim.*) And when the robbers had put the candle out . . . (*All hum in harmony. The donkey sneezes. The pyramid collapses. Music. A gigantic fight breaks out between the animals and the robbers. The robbers, banging heads, are knocked out. The animals search for each other in the darkness, quietly braying, barking, meowing, and crowing to the tune of the following lines from "Side by Side."*)

DONKEY

Oh, we ain't got a barrel of money,

CAT

Maybe we're ragged and funny,

DOG

But we'll travel along,

ROOSTER

  Singin' a song . . .
  (*Touching, they find one another. Now, singing the words, they*
  cautiously start dancing.)

ALL

  Side by side.

  Oh, we don't know what's comin' tomorrow,
  Maybe it's trouble and sorrow,
  But we'll travel the road,
  Sharin' the load,
  Side by side.

  Through all kinds of weather,
  What if the sky should fall . . .
  (*The robbers wake up. Both the animals and the robbers are*
  frightened. Then all begin to smile and join together in the song
  and dance. The lights come up.)
  Just as long as we're together,
  It doesn't matter at all.

  When they've all had their quarrels and parted,
  We'll be the same as we started,
  Just trav'lin' along,
  Singin' a song,
  Side by side.
  (*All exit, dancing. Blackout.*)

Production History

Fables Here and Then was conceived and developed under the direction of David Feldshuh. The play was first produced by The Guthrie Theater to tour forty-three cities in the Upper Midwest for nine weeks in the fall of 1971 under a grant from the Hill Family Foundation. Following the tour the play opened at The Guthrie Theater in Minneapolis on December 20, 1971.

Original Cast

Ross Bickell
Ivar Brogger
Lance Davis
Tovah Feldshuh
Katherine Ferrand
Erik Fredricksen
William Rhys, replacement actor during
the last week of the production

Music composed by Roberta Carlson
Sets and costumes by Ron Hall
Lighting by Robert Bye
Tour arranged and managed by David Hawkanson

The Centipede. The lizard, the goose, and the owl enjoy the centipede's dance. "How on earth do you know which foot to put down when?" (Photograph by John L. Anderson/theatre graphics.)

The Wise Man. The lazy man says, "I'll pull the tail." His wife replies, "I'll pull the pot." (Photograph by Lynn Ball.)

How the Snake Lost His Voice. The cricket pulls the voice out of the snake as if it were a long cord. The snake's voice gets lower and lower until he is left with just a hiss. (Photograph by Lynn Ball.)

How the Snake Lost His Voice. The earthworm searches blindly for something she will never find. (Photograph by John L. Anderson/theatre graphics.)

The Wise Man. At the market three roosters and a duck wait to be sold.
(Photograph by John L. Anderson/theatre graphics.)

The Bremen Town Musicians. So the dog said, "We ought to attack them." The donkey placed himself below the window, and the dog climbed upon the donkey's back, and the cock climbed upon the dog's shoulders, and the cat climbed upon the cock's shoulders, and they waited for the robbers to put out the candle. (Photograph by John L. Anderson/theatre graphics.)

The Shirt Collar. The soggy, dripping clothes are hung on the line to dry. (Photograph by Lynn Ball.)

Gassir the Hero. "The fighter and the fight disappear within the night of time — and leave only my song." The lights fade with the partridge standing above a humbled Gassir. (Photograph by Lynn Ball.)

The Fisherman and the Sea King's Daughter. Urashima dies as the fisherman sights something. "Look, out in the bay, the shadow of a man riding a giant turtle, and a beautiful silver fish leaping and swimming alongside!" (Photograph by John L. Anderson/theatre graphics.)

The Silver Bell. "What would the world be like if we all just danced and danced?" (Photograph by Lynn Ball.)

The Snake's Theme

NOTE: Music for *Fables Here and Then* composed by Roberta Carlson.
Copyright © 1974 by Roberta Carlson. All rights reserved.

Gassir the Hero

The Cookie Jar

John Clark Donahue

Respectfully dedicated to the memory of

Mahalia Jackson

Comments

The Cookie Jar is filled with cookie baking, gospel singing, jazz, soft-shoe dancing, and children's daydreams. It is also packed with conflicts between stale cake and homemade cookies, between Saturday morning TV villains and umbrella repairmen, and between chrome-plated commercial gadgetry and a life lived simply in an abandoned matchbox.

Cookie Land is a tiny country in a dirty spot on the bottom of an abandoned mixing bowl. Almost all its inhabitants have long since lost their recipes for baking cookies. They have learned to rely on the Stale Cake Company for all their needs; these media merchants have a monopoly on Cookie Land imaginations and pocketbooks. But not all the Cookie folk are impressed by the Stale Cake jargon — a few still sit on rooftops or in the stillness of a pea patch to sing and dream, and a few still have their recipes for home baking which they practice every day.

The chorus of the play is composed of the children and adults of the land who are more influenced by the hard sell of the Stale Cake Company than by the soft-spoken advocates of the simple life (Mother Mary, Wet Paint Bill, Old Glue Needle, and Winde). But when the chorus members yield to the commercial pitch, they discover that the products they buy are useless and that there is famine in the land.

217

Enraged, they begin to search for the Stale Cake Company, but in the Matchbox House the Cookie Land people and the Stale Cake Company learn the pleasure of sharing life's simple necessities with one another.

The play illustrates the polarity between the values of the Stale Cake Company and those of the Matchbox House people, and it encourages each member of the audience to decide which of the extremes is more influential in his or her own life. Nevertheless, it is not so much a "message" play or an intellectual puzzle as a medium for a shared theater event in which both actors and audience participate. The culmination of the event occurs when at the end of the play the actors pass cookies and lemonade through the audience, mingling informally with those who attend the play and inviting them onstage to sing and talk.

The play began as merely a title in 1971, a year before the script was written, while the staff members of the Children's Theatre Company of the Minneapolis Society of Fine Arts were planning the 1972 season. They insisted that John Donahue should create a new play for the coming season; he agreed and offered the title *The Cookie Jar* without having a specific theme in mind. The title, sans scenario, lay quietly in the back of Donahue's mind for a year until the actual writing began. Donahue prepared for writing and directing the show (activities which took place simultaneously) by watching Saturday morning children's television programs and trying to understand the effects the medium has on young imaginations and values.

"Most young people today are a great distance away from the kind of values that are represented by the group in the Matchbox House and are very much in tune with gold-plated swans in sunken bathrooms, shiny cars, lots of machinery in the kitchen and garage, a 'rec room,' and all that," Donahue believes. He was not surprised that many members of the audience found the Stale Cake Company very charming: "The Stale Cake Company and all of their accouterments and charms are, within the world in which they function, very powerful. If the orientation of the viewers is toward that pseudo-hip, chrome-plated thing that the Stale Cake Company represents, then they are going to like the Stale Cake Company better. There are suburbs filled with kids who wouldn't give a hoot for living in a matchbox with an old black woman and a couple of old bums, living very simply."

The people in the Matchbox House know this, too. Mother Mary tells the two children who are drawn to the simple life, Bubble and Black-Eyed Pea, "So maybe your old nose is just in fine shape to taste a cookie and know it's settin' fine. But don't you think, babies, that everybody sees it, 'cause there's plenty of people out there wantin' a portable whatever-it-is, just to make them feel happy." And Wet Paint Bill reminds them, "If you don't know what's good in the first place, how you gonna tell the difference when you see it? When it's lookin' you in the face?"

Mother Mary, Winde, Wet Paint Bill, and Black-Eyed Pea are all played by black actors. None of the members of the Stale Cake Company are black; the Oreo Cookie Man (the black community's slang name for the black person who is "black on the outside, white on the inside") is played by a white actor in blackface. Donahue does not suggest that all black people know how to live simply and happily — many of the confused members of the chorus are black, and the black teenagers who hold a jive session do not understand what motivates Black-Eyed Pea. But, Donahue observes, "The black man in this country has had to endure a very basic existence with his finger on values which were for him essential to his survival. He had to make do and has brilliantly endured and has, whether he really knows it or not, a sense of what he needs. This is not true of anybody one hundred percent, but when you haven't got much, you tend to know what you need." (As one song in the play advises, "Don't be grabbin' for more than you've got, just know that you've got what you need.") In contrast to this there are many individuals in our society who have grown up with everything, never knowing what they need and assembling around them all manner of paraphernalia. If there is a "message" in The Cookie Jar, it is a soft-pedaled plea for integration of black and white and for a common understanding among people who hold different values or who come from different economic backgrounds. Mother Mary suggests this when she counsels, "You've got to put it all together into one big bowl!"

Another theme in the play is the relationship of spiritual values to social and economic values. On the one hand, the god that the Stale Cake Company preaches about is a god who tells people they were put on earth to get all they can. On the other hand, Winde, the positive spiritual element in the play, observes and participates in the action of the story and inspires Mother Mary and Black-Eyed Pea to sing "Sweet Jesus, Precious Savior." In all of Donahue's original plays the Holy Spirit is an important figure; to Donahue it is the spiritual presence in an individual's life that allows one to transcend peer or societal influence and to find peace and harmony within himself. *The Cookie Jar* was produced for audiences in the Easter season, and the communion it creates for participants is a celebration of spiritual rebirth and renewal.

As Donahue made his decisions about which characters would represent positive and negative influences and which would represent the audience, the scenario began to take shape. He met frequently with the composer, Roberta Carlson, whose ideas for the musical statements and styles often dictated the lyrics or the form of a scene rather than vice versa. (In the end the music itself offers a satiric commentary on the commercialization of various musical styles and traditions.) The ideas for music and scenario were then presented to the actors, the production staff, and many of the teenagers in the school program of the Children's Theatre Company for their reactions and contributions. The scenario was amended and developed further throughout the formative period, and some of the songs were composed in part at the same time.

The dialogue was written as the play was rehearsed over a period of five weeks. Donahue usually sketched a scene during the day before it was rehearsed, then edited and developed it with the aid of the actors and the composer as the rehearsals progressed. "Jivin'" and "The Stale Cake Company at the Railway Station" were almost entirely improvised by the actors. The process of revision continued to the end of the rehearsal period, and some scenes were eliminated as late as the preview night. The musical score had to be completed several days before the opening of the play to give the musicians an opportunity to rehearse, but it too was created and revised in concert with the actors and the director.

The setting is a gigantic mixing bowl that fills the stage. The side of the bowl toward the audience is represented only by the rim, which soars and curves from one side of the proscenium to the other. The rim is supported by a ladder and a giant matchstick. The surface of the bowl is painted to look like an old fence or a billboard covered with ragged remnants of old posters and paintings. At upstage right the bowl is partially cut away; in the "Famine" scene this section is backlighted with red to create an inferno effect. A rope ladder and wooden pegs are affixed to the surface of the bowl to allow children to climb on it. Black velours are hung upstage of the bowl. The openings on either side of the bowl are curtained with red cloth that is gathered to suggest entrances to a circus tent.

The Matchbox House is a giant matchbox lying on its side. The drawer of the matchbox slides across the stage to reveal a jumble of matches from which hang clothing, lamps, pots, and pans. A slide behind the matchbox lid provides one entrance to the house. The only "furniture" in the house consists of an overstuffed armchair, a painter's easel, and an ironing board that has been made into a piano keyboard. In the 1973 production of the play the company substituted a giant umbrella for the matchbox. The umbrella lay on its side on a rolling platform, and the household was arranged on the platform in the shelter of the umbrella. The umbrella proved to be an efficient stage device, especially for touring purposes.

The costumes are contemporary. The Stale Cake Company's costumes are meant to be as garish and tasteless as their routines and their behavior. Mother Mary, Bubble, Black-Eyed Pea, Wet Paint Bill, and Old Glue Needle dress in clothes that are timeless, simple, and unpretentious.

The Cookie Jar is the eighth original play written and directed by John Donahue for the Children's Theatre Company, and it is the fifth of his plays for families and children. The eight are (in the order in which they were produced) *Good Morning, Mr. Tillie* (1966, 1970); *Hang On to Your Head* (1967, 1972); *Variations on a Similar Theme, an Homage to René Magritte* (for adults; 1967, 1972); *Old Kieg of Malfi* (1968); *How Could You Tell?* (1969); *A Wall* (a play for adults which took its inspiration from a scenario by Alvin Greenberg; 1971);

The Cookie Jar (1972, 1973); and *The Netting of the Troupial* (for adults; 1973). Donahue also wrote the libretto for Dominick Argento's opera *A Postcard from Morocco* (which Donahue directed) for the Minnesota Opera Company in the fall of 1971. The libretto originated from Donahue's one-act play *The Suitcase,* which is one of the playlets in *Variations on a Similar Theme. The Suitcase* was also developed into a screenplay and was filmed in color in June, 1973.

In all of his writing and directing Donahue is concerned with the contrast between an artist's own esthetic values and the mediocre artistic values that are widely approved by the society to which he belongs; Donahue observes that this contrast often results in conflict between the two and alienation of the artist. *The Cookie Jar* examines the Stale Cake values that the mass media sell to a gullible public, and it suggests that these values may be of dubious worth. However, Donahue cautions, "It is not *too* idealistic. After all, the whole thing is really about cookies."

Linda Walsh Jenkins
Editor

The Cookie Jar

Characters

Bubble .... A young boy

Winde .... The presence of God, the Holy Spirit

Black-Eyed Pea .... A teenaged black girl

Old Glue Needle, Wet
   Paint Bill, and
   Mother Mary .... Inhabitants of the Matchbox House

Members of the Stale Cake Company:

   Daddy Tutti-Fruit Hat.. A combination of ringmaster, disc
                                                        jockey, and used car salesman

   Diana Dumbstrut ...... A brassy blond cheerleader, the
                                                        advertising world's sexy female

   Dorothy Doughie ...... An aging parody of Shirley Temple
                                                        as a child star

   Oreo Cookie Man ..... A white man in blackface with an
                                                        Afro wig

   Captain Steal .... A hippie rock star with a wooden leg

   Electric Piggybank Man No one knows if he is a pig that
                                                        turned into a man or a man who
                                                        turned into a pig. He rides a tricycle
                                                        which pulls the Dream Wagon, a
                                                       vehicle vaguely resembling the small
                                                       cart used by an ice cream vendor. The
                                                       Dream Wagon contains gadgets,
                                                       props, and toys.

   People of Cookie Land ... Approximately twenty children,
                                                        teenagers, and adults

Sequence of Scenes

Prologue   Children Playing

As the musicians in the orchestra play a lyrical jazz set, small children crawl, climb, wander, and play on the stage, swinging on ropes and climbing along the rim of the mixing bowl. Mother Mary enters and sits with a storybook in a big armchair. The children sit at her feet, and she reads to them. The mottled lighting and the music create a dreamlike atmosphere; the audience cannot hear Mother Mary over the music. It is as though the audience were privy to a memory of the scene.

Scene i   "Bake a Cookie for Me!"

Theme: "Bake a Cookie for Me!" The lights change to a warm pool on Mother Mary and the children.

MOTHER MARY

Once upon a time in a place called Cookie Land, there lived an old lady. But afore I tell you about this old lady, I'm goin' to tell you sumpin' about Cookie Land. Now they called this place Cookie Land 'cause it was the only thing they had for to live on, was cookies! 'Course they had every kind of cookies in this land, for instance, they had . . . ooohh, ahhhh, lettuce cookies, mashed potatoes cookies, grits cookies, and so on. They had winter stockin' cookies, so they didn't get cold in the feet. Now then, anyway, this old lady went to the kitchen to get a coconut macaroon cookie that she had baked a long time ago. But when she got up in the cupboard by way of an old rickety ladder, built for her by her husband before he died — a loony death — out on the front lawn in the middle of a hailstorm, well, anyway, this tired old lady . . .

CHILD

A witch?

MOTHER MARY

No, not a witch, just a tired old lady . . . anyhow, she went to the cupboard and reached into the cookie jar, and all she found was a hard-as-a-rock raisin and a dead mouse.

CHILD

What happened?

MOTHER MARY

She died. She starved to death in three days because she forgot the recipe. Some kids in the neighborhood found her dead on the kitchen floor. And written in flour under the sink was this message: "Bake a cookie for me!" . . . Did you like that? (*The children smile and nod. She hugs them, and they talk quietly as the lights fade.*)

Scene ii   The Stale Cake
Company and Bubble

The lights come up on Winde, sweeping and singing in the street. He speaks to the audience.

WINDE

Hello. This is the main street of Cookie Land, and I am in charge of sweeping the crumbs off of the pavement. But occasionally one or two slip by me . . . Like now! (*Boogie theme: "The Wooden Spoon Hop." The inhabitants of Cookie Land and the members of the Stale Cake Company make their entrances in a choreographed sequence. Most are teenagers dressed in contemporary style but not exaggeratedly so. They wear gold paper crowns, many chew gum, some wave cheerleaders' pompoms. Their gestures and movements possess the artless vulgarity seen in some television choreography. The Cookie Land people begin to arrive and to greet the Stale Cake Company. The Electric Piggybank Man pushes in Diana Dumbstrut, who rides on a workman's dolly; she is swathed in cellophane and is flanked by a giant plastic fork and spoon. She looks like a cheap plastic doll sold at a discount store. She steps through the cellophane, blows a whistle, does a drum majorette's backbend, then dances to the side. The people scream and cheer. Dorothy Doughie and the Oreo Cookie Man enter. They do brief dances that are associated with their roles throughout the play and join Diana Dumbstrut. Captain Steal enters with a huge poster which he unfurls. It reads "Stale Cake Company," with the lettering in the style of a Coca-Cola sign. Two girls carry the sign upstage and hold it there to frame the action at center stage as Captain Steal joins the others. Finally, Daddy Tutti-Fruit Hat enters and displays a sign that reads "Cookie Trip — Win!! Just Bake It." He strides over to the assembled crowd.*)

229

DADDY TUTTI-FRUIT HAT

(*in the oily voice of a disc jockey*) Hi, kids!

CHILDREN

Hi!

DADDY TUTTI-FRUIT HAT

How's every little thing?

CHILDREN

Fine!

DADDY TUTTI-FRUIT HAT

Far out! You know, you kids really take the cake! (*As he says this, he lifts his whip above his head and freezes at the end of the sentence. Everyone onstage freezes except Bubble. The lights dim on them, leaving only a pool of light on Bubble, who is seated downstage on the rim of the bowl-world. A flute is heard.*)

BUBBLE

Hello. You know, come to think of it . . . I am not too happy with the way things are in my life, and I'm not very old yet either, nine or so. Yesterday I made this little flute out of sticks . . . it doesn't really play, but it's like I saw in a picture once . . . I wish I played the flute or something . . . I have a snapshot of my Uncle Steve playing the fiddle at a picnic but that was before me and I never heard it . . . Anyway, so much is happening to confuse a person these days . . . certain kinds of birds dying out, people building fences in their yards to keep out something. Kids fighting over who's got the best color . . . bike or not. My dad said I couldn't plant corn and sunflowers in the backyard 'cause it was too much trouble and tracked in dirt, my ma said . . . I think I'll dress up in a leaf suit and climb up in a tree and stay there, dressed in my leaf suit, forever . . . at least the wind and I'd have a lot to agree upon. (*The lights come up suddenly as the others onstage snap back into action.*)

DADDY TUTTI-FRUIT HAT

All right, kids!

ELECTRIC PIGGYBANK MAN

(*pointing to Bubble and oinking for Daddy Tutti-Fruit Hat's attention*) Oink! Oink! Oink!

DADDY TUTTI-FRUIT HAT

Heeeyyy! Heeeyyyy! (*He goes to Bubble.*) What are ya doin' up there? Come on down here, fast! (*Bubble jumps into his arms.*) What do you need, huh? What do you need? (*Daddy Tutti-Fruit Hat shoves Bubble into the group of children.*)

SHEILA

Hey, what's the matter with you? Didn't you know the Stale Cake Company was in town?

MATT

Yeah, man, they're neato, keeno!

RICKY

They're the coolest, man!

BARRY

What's the matter with you?

KIM

Yeah, get with it.

DADDY TUTTI-FRUIT HAT

All right, kids, here it is! The Portable Key Toast Hat! (*He puts a toaster-hat device on his head, pulls a cord, and plastic wedges pop up. The children scream and cheer.*) Only $7.95 in toy departments everywhere. Put it right on your head, pull the little strap down. Pops 'em right up, huh? Is that beautiful? Is that far out or what?

DIANA DUMBSTRUT

You can have a hot waffle any time when you wear this hat.

DADDY TUTTI-FRUIT HAT

All right, sweetheart, step right up here! (*to the others*) Get back! All right, you . . . (*He pulls one of the girls from the crowd.*) What's your name, darling?

BRIDGET

Bridget!

DADDY TUTTI-FRUIT HAT

How old are you, Bridget?

BRIDGET

Eleven. (*She squirms and waves to her friends; she is chewing gum and her speech is barely intelligible.*)

DADDY TUTTI-FRUIT HAT

Eleven . . . Bridget, would you like to pull the Portable Key Toast cord?

BRIDGET

Yeah!

DADDY TUTTI-FRUIT HAT

Go ahead, give it a little tug. (*Bridget barely touches it.*) That's enough! (*He pushes her away.*) All right, Bridget, for your test, I'm going to see if you can do the "Wooden Spoon Hop"! All right, let's everyone snap your fingers and help Bridget out! (*The children snap their fingers in rhythm. Bridget does an absurd dance step reminiscent of the "Mashed Potato." The children yell "Sad!" "Far out!" and similar slang jargon. Daddy Tutti-Fruit Hat stops Bridget's dance.*) Isn't she far out? Here's a couple of tickets to the big show, sweetheart! OK, guys and gals, boys and girls, swingers! Here we go with another far out rendition of the Stale Cake Company theme song! (*Theme: "The Stale Cake Company." As Daddy Tutti-Fruit Hat sings, the Stale Cake Company and the children sing a 1950s rock "oooohhhh!" background. They sway in the dance style of the 1950s.*)

It's the real thing, it's the true thing,
It's a love thing, it's a good thing,
It's a God thing, it's a stale thing!

STALE CAKE COMPANY

Lemme tell ya!

DADDY TUTTI-FRUIT HAT

You can get it and we're here to tell you how!

STALE CAKE COMPANY

Oh, ya need it!

DADDY TUTTI-FRUIT HAT

You can get it and it's waiting right here,
If you only come and . . .

DADDY TUTTI-FRUIT HAT and STALE CAKE COMPANY

Buy, buy, buy!

(*The children cheer and whistle.*)

DADDY TUTTI-FRUIT HAT

Far out. That was really beautiful, you guys. I'm going to take off the Portable Key Toast Hat and put back on the Daddy Tutti-Fruit Hat, because it's serious time now, kids . . . (*underscore: "The Stale Cake Company"*) I'm going to tell you a little story, a story of truth and meaning for modern man in these troubled times, and you boys and girls, too . . . I'm going to tell you of a woman who came to me in dire distress. She did not know what to do. Her life was a shambles, her marriage was on the rocks, her husband drank heavily because of an accident at work, and her daughter was a bummer at school. *And* she had just lost her blouse. She did not know what to do. She came to me and she said, "Daddy Tutti-Fruit Hat, I do not know what to do, but I read your ad in this comic book and I just hope that you can help me out." And I said, "My dear, I am Daddy Tutti-Fruit Hat, are I not?" And she said, "Yes, you are." And I said, "My dear, here you take this, free of charge on a thirty-day free trial, money-back guarantee, the Stale Cake Company's very own Franges Dober Flutter, $11.95 at toy departments everywhere (*speaking rapidly*) requires seven-Eveready-Triple-A-Penlight-batteries-batteries-not-included." Well, she took it home and the next day she came back to me and she said, "Daddy Tutti-Fruit Hat, God came to me last night, and He said, 'I put you on this earth to get everything you can, and the Stale Cake Company is there to help you get it!'" From that day on, she got everything that she could. She went downtown and she got and she got and she bought and she bought and she got and she bought and she bought and she got. Her husband got his job back! (*The members of the Stale Cake Company and a few of the children call out as if in response to a revival testimonial: "Yeah!" "Tell 'em!" "Right on!"*) He stopped drinking. She found her lost blouse. And her daughter became far out.

ALL

(*yelling*) Far out!

DADDY TUTTI-FRUIT HAT

Her daughter became right on!

ALL

Right on!

DADDY TUTTI-FRUIT HAT

Her daughter became . . . Miss Diana Dumbstrut, the Girl with the Golden Goose! Here she is, the living testimony! (*Percussion accompanies Daddy Tutti-Fruit Hat's introduction of Diana Dumbstrut. Daddy Tutti-Fruit Hat steps aside and gestures toward Diana Dumbstrut in the manner of an announcer introducing a nightclub act. The children shriek and cheer as she steps into the spotlight. She leans back into a drum majorette pose, nearly falls, then stands and poses. She is the dumb blond stereotype: She cannot talk very well, her voice is shrill, she twitches, her eggbeater baton slips over her eye, and her fake eyelashes make her appear cross-eyed. She constantly wears a Miss America smile and keeps glancing over at Daddy Tutti-Fruit Hat to see how she is doing.*)

DIANA DUMBSTRUT

I was no one . . . and nobody knew who I was. I had nothing, and then I met Daddy Tutti-Fruit Hat and the Stale Cake Company, and they told me this, which I will remember to this very day. They said to me, "Go out and get. Get all you can!" And so I got and I got and I bought and I bought. I bought my suit, and the Franges Dober Flutter, and my baton, and now, I am . . . Diana Dumbstrut! (*All cheer.*)

DADDY TUTTI-FRUIT HAT

Isn't she far out! (*All cheer.*) Isn't she right on!

ALL

Right on! (*Diana Dumbstrut returns to the Stale Cake Company. Daddy Tutti-Fruit Hat takes the spotlight again.*)

DADDY TUTTI-FRUIT HAT

Thanks very much, Diana, you're a sweetheart. All right, boys and girls, I know you're anxious to try out your own Portable Key Toast Hat and your own Franges Dober Flutter! (*The children cheer after each item is mentioned.*) And your recipe for the Mini Cookie! (*He ad-libs the names of other products.*) But first I'm going to ask Diana Dumbstrut, the Girl with the Golden Goose, to lead us down the street in a parade. (*Theme: "The Stale Cake Company." They march out with Diana Dumbstrut leading. Bubble is left sitting on the stage, watching them go. Winde comes onstage from the audience, sweeping.*)

WINDE

Hey, what you got there?

BUBBLE

It's a little flute, but it's not real.

WINDE

Let me see it. Did you make it yourself?

BUBBLE

Yeah.

WINDE

That's pretty good! You know something? You're going to learn to play that flute someday.

BUBBLE

I hope so. (*Boogie theme: "The Wooden Spoon Hop." Daddy Tutti-Fruit Hat and several children dance across the stage. Daddy Tutti-Fruit Hat gestures for Bubble to join them, but Bubble just watches. The lights fade down.*)

Scene iii   Bubble and Winde

As the lights come up slowly, Bubble runs onstage with an umbrella, climbs the ladder hurriedly, and sits on the rim of the bowl-world downstage. Thunder. Offstage, a voice calls faintly. Bubble opens the umbrella and curls up underneath it to sing and daydream. A girl is leaning against the proscenium, and a boy is sitting, his chin in his hands and his elbows propped on his knees, on a rung of the ladder. The girl sings with Bubble, and the boy, getting up and moving away from the ladder, speaks some of the lines of the song to emphasize the images.

BUBBLE and GIRL
>   (*singing*)
>>   *Once I was a bubble . . .*

BOY
>   Once I was a bubble . . .

BUBBLE and GIRL
>   (*singing*)
>>   *On the rushing water stream . . .*

BOY
>   On the rushing water stream . . .

BUBBLE and GIRL
>   (*singing*)
>>   *A sailing ball . . .*

BOY
>   A sailing ball . . .

BUBBLE and GIRL
>   (*singing*)
>>   *A magic sea ship,*
>>   *A window for a fish.*

BOY
>   . . . A window for a fish.

(*Winde enters on a bicycle during the song. He wears a farmer's straw hat and carries a sprinkling can in the bicycle basket. He rides between the girl and the boy to the ladder and joins in the singing.*)

BUBBLE, GIRL, and WINDE
>   (*singing*)
>>   *We played a while, then rolled and tumbled,*
>>   *The bubble and the wave,*
>>   *Two glass clowns from a water show,*
>>   *Two clear spring days . . .*

(*The boy who spoke wanders away, lost in his own daydreams now, and exits.*)

>>   *Each juggling river drops*
>>   *On the tips of wet fingers,*
>>   *When I awoke, the river dry, its bed my own,*
>>   *But I, my hair still salt wet, my pillow*

Still dream sweet.

(*The girl drifts away and exits.*)

WINDE

That's quite a story.

BUBBLE

Yes, but how did you know it, too? You sang right along with me.

WINDE

Well, you know, I think I had that same dream myself when I was your age. In fact, I still have it now . . . some days.

BUBBLE

Gosh! Who are you, anyway?

WINDE

Today I'm taking care of the flowers, tryin' to bring a little sunshine and a little soft rain to them. (*During this exchange two young girls bring potted plants to Winde, who examines the plants, waters them carefully, and shares a smile with each girl. The girls exit.*) They could use it, you know. Boy, this summer's been hot.

BUBBLE

Wow! It sure has. You're a gardener, I suppose.

WINDE

Oooohhh . . . some days.

BUBBLE

I'd like that job . . . I think.

WINDE

Some days . . . you probably would. Try it sometime.

BUBBLE

Yeah. But I thought I saw you working in the street, yesterday, sweeping.

WINDE

Some days.

BUBBLE

Oh! I see . . . part-time here and part-time there, sort of . . . You work part-time. You've got more than one job. Part-time here and part-time there.

WINDE

> Well . . . that's one way to put it . . . or maybe all over the place . . . a little bit . . . all the time.

BUBBLE

> Hmmm. (*He thinks about it.*) What's your name?

WINDE

> (*pause*) Wind . . . -e; Winde.

BUBBLE

> Well, 'bye, Winde, gotta go home now. There's a robin building a nest in the backyard in our hedge. So anyway, I got this box of string and stuff that I'm goin' to throw in the grass . . . in case he needs it. 'Bye! (*He blows on the stick flute. Suddenly it works and he is astonished. Flute.*) Wow! (*He heads down the ladder and says "Wow!" again. He jumps on Winde's bike and rides off blowing his flute as the orchestra picks up the fluting and makes a transition into wind sounds.*)

Scene iv   Jivin'

Theme: "Jivin' Boogie." This scene was improvised by the black teenagers of the Children's Theatre Company, and it is offered as an example, not as a set script. The teenagers created the dialogue and jokes out of their own shared vocabulary and references. The names used were those of the actors. The setting is a jive session among friends.

KIM

> Here's the way Mr. Johnson walks: he's a teacher at our school. Here's the way he walks, tryin' to walk the way we do. Chicka boom, chicka boom, chicka boom boom boom . . . (*Laughter. Everyone talks at once as Kim minces across the stage. Kim mimics Mr. Johnson.*) Uh, give me five, sister. (*The teenagers laugh; each tries to top the other.*)

ARTIE

Guess what, Garry, yesterday in school we had a vote . . .

GARRY

So . . .

ARTIE

You won.

GARRY

Won what?

ARTIE

Out!

GARRY

Out?

ARTIE

O-U-T! (*All laugh and gesture freely throughout the scene, appreciating one another's jokes; friendly battles develop.*)

KEVIN

Speaking of Garry, I saw Garry walkin' down the street, and these other black people were walkin' the other way. So Garry started sayin', "Black is beautiful! Black is beautiful!" And one of the black dudes stopped, looked at Garry, and said, "Wait, we got to talk about this one!"

GARRY

Well, did Kevin tell you that him and his brothers were going to get on the bus the other day? They didn't have the fare to pay so the driver took them to the back . . .

ALL

To the back!

GARRY

Put some paper down . . .

ALL

Put some paper down . . .

GARRY

And put them on some chairs and said, "Don't make a dirty pit back here." In other words, you are a dog!

DAVID

Wait, everybody, one of these days I am going to be rich!

ALL

> Sad!

DAVID

> I'm going to have a rich car, a rich house, a rich woman, and a rich phone. And I'm going to call you, and you, and maybe you two over there, and I'm going to dial and say, "Ding a ling."

ALL

> Hello!

DAVID

> I'm sorry, but you got the wrong number — and I'm going to hang up!

NANCE

> When you get rich! Honey, you're so poor now, you can't even afford nothing free!

GARRY

> Wait a minute, everybody, shut up! When I get rich, like he just said, I'm going to walk in front of the TV set, and the band will be playin' behind me. And I'm going to tell you (*looking at Kim*) to turn your set off, 'cause I'm too good to be looked at and might blind your eyes.

KIM

> Honey, I hate to say it, but you're going to have to pay them to get on that TV set.

GARRY

> They've got to pay you to get off!!! Cockroach face! (*The "Jivin' Boogie" theme picks up underneath.*)

KIM

> Yeah, well, I went over to Garry's house, which they purchased through S and H Gold Bond stamps. And I went up to the house, which looked like somebody's back alley. I walked up to the refrigerator . . .

NANCE

> Ah-ah . . . icebox, honey.

DAVID

> No, you mean cooler.

KEVIN

No way . . . you mean picnic basket.

KIM

I walked up to the picnic basket, looked in, and I saw cockroaches inside, dancin' around, and they had signs. You know why? 'Cause they were on strike. And do you know what they were doing? They were singing; here's what they were singing . . .

ALL

(*singing*)
We done overcome,
We sho' had some fun . . .

GARRY

That's all right, Miss Tons of Fun. I came over to your house, which you got at Pay Less Shoes. Knocked on the door, which fell apart afterwards, and a cockroach came and said, "Hat and coat, please." I said, "Sho', honey, but where's your master?" And them cockroaches were fat and greasy.

KEVIN

Hold on, everybody, I got a joke. See there was this black man and this white man on the bus . . .

DAVID

Wait, Kevin, I think I figured out why you tell so many racial jokes . . . 'Cause you *are* a racial joke. (*Kevin and David start arguing; Nance stops them.*)

NANCE

Ah, be quiet and listen to me, Kevin. Your racial jokes are so funky that when you moved into your neighborhood the neighbors' grass died!

KEVIN

Yeah, you know what I heard? I heard that if you put your brain on a razor blade, it would look like a BB rolling down a four-lane highway. Now beat that!

KIM

Oh, Garry, guess what . . .

GARRY

Shut up, Big Lips!

KIM

Y'all heard of banjo eyes, have ya? Well, you're looking at banjo lips. Why, his lips is so big that his mother had to make him a lip case, and on the cover she put his nickname.

NANCE

What was it, honey?

KIM

"Chopper" . . . Not only that, but at night he has to wear a lip brace, so his lips won't fall out of the bed.

GARRY

Honey, I hate to tell you that your nickname is Rotunda Lips, Bongo Lips, Raw Steak Lips . . . (*He ad-libs.*) Your friends just said that you had two big disaster areas on the lower part of your face. Meaning your big baggy watermelon lips. (*He changes the subject.*) Now show me what you've got in that sack.

KIM

I went downtown the other day, by ghetto express . . .

GARRY

Your family owns it.

KIM

Yeah! That's why you walk so much. Hey, I heard that blonds have more fun . . .

NANCE

Who told you that?

KIM

Well, I decided to cash in on some of that fun that I have been missing out on. (*She takes a blond wig from the sack and begins strutting across the stage. Garry snatches the wig, puts it on, and does an imitation of a white blond "swinger." Others begin dancing. Garry throws the wig on the floor and dances in up-to-date black style. Everyone joins in, laughing and talking, until the music stops abruptly.*) There was a soul food dinner at our school the other day.

ARTIE

What did they have?

KIM

Black-eyed peas.

ALL

And do you know what them black-eyed peas was?

GARRY

Pork 'n' beans burnt on one side. (*The music resumes. The teenagers dance and continue "jivin'," then they turn upstage and dance toward the wall of the bowl. Black-Eyed Pea enters, carrying her parasol, and walks through them to a pool of light at the center.*)

Scene v   Black-Eyed Pea

There is a clash of cymbals; the music stops and the teenagers freeze.

BLACK-EYED PEA

Yeah, things began to change and I stopped hanging around with those other kids, and when girls would call me up I'd say I was sick or somethin'. Instead I go up on the roof by the chimney and just sit up there and listen. (*The other teenagers speak lines out of the darkness upstage.*)

GARRY

To what?

BLACK-EYED PEA

I heard this voice saying or kind of singing . . . all the time . . . !

STEPHANIE

So?

BLACK-EYED PEA

So . . . one night I went out and I looked for it. It was late, morning, in fact . . . I guess, but still dark . . . my feet wet and catching sick, maybe . . . So I put on this old pair of yellow overshoes, I don't know whose they were, they were in the garage . . . they looked like (*underscore: "Sweet Jesus, Precious Savior"**) fireman's or fishing boots or something . . . I was walking in the street . . . They sounded like a tin bells machine or I don't know . . . When I walked, I made little rhythms as I went . . . and I remember humming "Sweet Jesus, Precious Savior," slushing out a rubber dance against the curb. (*The others softly hum the song.*)

STEPHANIE

What happened?

BLACK-EYED PEA

I never saw anybody else. It was like I was walking through a model or something . . . you know? . . . and no sound except the buckles playing on my boots. No cars . . . no dogs . . . no doors shutting . . . no whistles . . . only . . . just me . . . my voice . . . my breath . . . my feet crunch . . . my pockets . . . my parade walk . . . music only. And the long low cry, cooing . . . begging . . . "Come on home, child . . . come on home . . . come on home to the kitchen table." (*She sings to the tune of "Sweet Jesus, Precious Savior."*)

> *Come on home*
> *To the kitchen, kitchen table . . .*
> *Come on . . .*

(*Bubble enters, carrying his umbrella. He walks to her and stands watching her.*)

BUBBLE

To the kitchen table?

BLACK-EYED PEA

Yeah.

BUBBLE

Did this voice say anything about cookies?

BLACK-EYED PEA

Cookies! What you mean cookies? What ya talkin'! . . . Cookies!

BUBBLE

Well, you said "kitchen," didn't you?

*Music on page 300.

BLACK-EYED PEA

Yeah.

BUBBLE

You bake cookies in the kitchen, don't you?

BLACK-EYED PEA

Yeah. Here I am talkin' voices and singin' and you're talkin' cookies! I'll bake *your* cookie! (*laughing*) What's your name, puppy? What's your name, puppy chil'?

BUBBLE

Bubble.

BLACK-EYED PEA

Bubble! Your name?

BUBBLE

Yes.

BLACK-EYED PEA

You mean people call you by "Bubble"? (*She laughs.*)

BUBBLE

Yes.

BLACK-EYED PEA

Sad! (*out of her laughter*) I'm a black-eyed pea.

BUBBLE

What?

BLACK-EYED PEA

Are you deaf?

BUBBLE

What?

BLACK-EYED PEA

I said, are you deaf?

BUBBLE

What?

BLACK-EYED PEA

He's deaf! I said, you're the bubble, I'm the black-eyed pea!

BUBBLE

Wow! You're the first other person I ever met without a regular name. How'd ya get it? Is that your real name?

BLACK-EYED PEA

'Course not. Is Bubble yours?

BUBBLE

Well, no!

BLACK-EYED PEA

Well then, hush up and shut your face . . . (*She laughs.*)
Hey . . . you play that thing? (*She points to his flute.*)

BUBBLE

No! Well . . . (*He remembers the sound.*)

BLACK-EYED PEA

Huh?

BUBBLE

Well, I guess so.

BLACK-EYED PEA

Well, play it! (*He blows on it. Flute sounds are heard.*) Sit down.
I'm going to tell you a little story here. (*Theme: "Black-Eyed
Pea."* Black-Eyed Pea sings the verses and choruses with great
freedom and ease.*)

> *In summer when the air is heavy breath,*
> *And the butterfly can float upon its back,*
> *I used to hide deep in the pea patch*
> *And listen to the warm ground breathing back.*
> *And I'd wonder how the earth it got so black.*

> *Black-Eyed Pea, Black-Eyed Pea,*
> *If you're wonderin' where this song comes from,*
> *Then take a look at me.*
> (Repeat refrain.)

> *In summer I'd pick the blossoms from the pea vine*
> *And wind them through my hair.*
> *And then I'd scoop the black dirt up*
> *And toss it everywhere.*
> *I musta been blessing the pea patch*
> *'Cause it was quiet and holy there.*

*Music on page 301.

Black-Eyed Pea, Black-Eyed Pea,
If you're wonderin' where this song comes from,
Then take a look at me.
(Repeat refrain.)

Later on in the summer, when the peas were ready to eat,
I went down to the pea patch, the air was smelling sweet.
I gazed into the garden and there to my surprise,
The pea patch I saw before my eyes was a pea patch in disguise.
Instead the leaves were silver wings and the pods were slippers fine.
And the waters from the rain before were jewels upon the vine.
I was the ruler of the kingdom, my subjects were so fine.
If you want a favor from me, just ask me any time.

Black-Eyed Pea, Black-Eyed Pea,
If you're wonderin' what to call me,
Just call me "Your Majesty."
(Repeat refrain.)

(*laughing*) No. I made that up. But anyway, I was always out in the back patch. So that's what they called me after a while, all the time, Black-Eyed Pea. That's how I got my name.

BUBBLE

Black-Eyed Pea . . .

BLACK-EYED PEA

Yes, Bubble . . .

BUBBLE

Can I be your friend?

BLACK-EYED PEA

Well, I guess you'd better be. (*They laugh. The "Bubble and Black-Eyed Pea" vamp begins. Bubble and Black-Eyed Pea walk in place in tempo through the next exchange, until the thunder sounds. They walk facing the audience like a vaudeville comic duo in a patter routine.*)

BUBBLE

Black-Eyed Pea, do you like cars?

BLACK-EYED PEA

Nope.

BUBBLE

Not even big long shiny red ones that go fast?

BLACK-EYED PEA

Nope.

BUBBLE

Do you like . . . TV?

BLACK-EYED PEA

Nope.

BUBBLE

To sing?

BLACK-EYED PEA

Yup.

BUBBLE

Dancin'?

BLACK-EYED PEA

Yup.

BUBBLE

Doin' the dishes? (*Black-Eyed Pea breaks out of the vamp step. The music stops.*)

BLACK-EYED PEA

Nope. 'Less I cook, then I do them. I take 'em and break 'em and throw them out the window. Better watch out, puppy, I'll break you! (*She laughs. The music resumes and she returns to the vamp pattern.*) Bubble, do you like grits?

BUBBLE

Never heard of 'em.

BLACK-EYED PEA

You better, honey, if you gonna be my friend. (*Pause. The music stops.*) How 'bout black?

BUBBLE

Well . . . maybe. (*in a tiny voice*) White?

BLACK-EYED PEA

>We'll see.

BLACK-EYED PEA and BUBBLE

>God? (*Thunder. Lights flash. The two children look at one another in astonishment.*)

BLACK-EYED PEA

>Come on, we're gonna get rained on. (*They run out, holding hands.*)

Scene vi   Old Glue Needle and Wet Paint Bill

Bubble and Black-Eyed Pea enter from one side of the stage and collide with Diana Dumbstrut and the Stale Cake Company coming from the other side.

DADDY TUTTI-FRUIT HAT

>Hey, kids, where ya been? We missed you. Where's your recipes for the Goodie Cookie and the Big Magic Cookie Pan Winner Pie? (*to Black-Eyed Pea*) Where's your queen crown, baby?

OREO COOKIE MAN

>What's the matter, honey? Did your mammy call you home?

CAPTAIN STEAL

>(*to Bubble*) Hey, little fella, you need your spaced beamer helmet with the built-in, far out pockets for cheat notes!

STALE CAKE COMPANY

>(*chanting a football yell with Diana Dumbstrut as the cheerleader*) Well! Come! On! Kids! Get! With! It! (*Black-Eyed Pea and Bubble hesitate in silence.*)

BUBBLE

>Well, what do you have?

STALE CAKE COMPANY

>(*chanting*) What! Do! We! Have! (*Theme: "The Stale Cake Com-*

pany." The members of the Stale Cake Company croon the
background as Daddy Tutti-Fruit Hat sings.)

DADDY TUTTI-FRUIT HAT

It's a real thing, it's a love thing,
It's a god thing, it's a . . .

BUBBLE

Have you got any flutes or lutes? (*The Stale Cake Company peo-*
ple don't know what he means; they ad-lib and mumble nerv-
ously.)

BLACK-EYED PEA

Any directions for making friends with fishes?

CAPTAIN STEAL

I've got a few ideas about that. (*The others motion for him to say*
no more.)

BUBBLE

Do you give lessons in shoemaking? I'd like to make myself a pair
of boots. (*Diana Dumbstrut shows her boots. Bubble shakes his*
head.)

BLACK-EYED PEA

Do you bake your own bread, Miss Doughie? I'd just love to have
a recipe for some of that bread. (*As Black-Eyed Pea turns away,*
Dorothy Doughie gestures as if to hit Black-Eyed Pea with her
spoon but is stopped by the others. The Stale Cake Company is
growling, becoming very hostile.)

BUBBLE

Can you skip stones? (*Members of the Stale Cake Company, out-*
raged, mutter: "Sk . . . sk . . . sk . . ." "What?")

BLACK-EYED PEA

Do you have any seeds?

DADDY TUTTI-FRUIT HAT

Aaaaaahhhhh! You mean Super Socko Space Steamin' Silver-
Coated One-A-Days . . . (*He pulls a pill bottle out of his coat.*)

BUBBLE

No! Just vegetable seeds. I'd like to have a little garden by my
back door . . . Do you have any rutabaga seeds? (*Members of*
the Stale Cake Company mutter: "Root . . . roo . . . tabay . . ."

"Cake . . ." "Seed . . ." "Roota . . .") Or maybe celery or carrots if you don't have rutabagas.

BLACK-EYED PEA

You got any directions in that wagon on how to grow black-eyed peas? (*Bubble and Black-Eyed Pea laugh. The members of the Stale Cake Company are bewildered.*) No? Then you take one bag of black dirt and some water, a hoe, one rake, and then seeds and some cow pie. You must have plenty of cow pie around here, Miss Doughie. (*Bubble and Black-Eyed Pea laugh. This infuriates the Stale Cake Company people. They growl and chomp, cartoon fashion.*)

DADDY TUTTI-FRUIT HAT

Hey, I guess we'll have to teach you two a lesson. You kids don't seem to know what's good for you in life. You don't know what you need to live. We'll make you kids rich and fat! Cute and glamorous!

DOROTHY DOUGHIE

Strong and rich!

OREO COOKIE MAN

We'll give you kids linoleum shoes with shiny fingers!

DIANA DUMBSTRUT

Gold jet pants!

CAPTAIN STEAL

Doll sets that swim in the sink!

ELECTRIC PIGGYBANK MAN

A bike with parties inside!

DADDY TUTTI-FRUIT HAT

And fat red candy face electric cow silver eggbeaters! (*As he says this, the members of the Stale Cake Company turn on the two children and begin to chase them in slow motion, brandishing their props as clubs, growling and sneering. As they chase the children, Old Glue Needle and Wet Paint Bill enter with their umbrella-repairing wagon, which they push to the center of the stage. The group comes circling toward them; the two rest calmly against the wagon and the children run past them. The children*

*then sit down, downstage of the two men, and the Stale Cake
Company people halt suddenly, staring at the newcomers.*)

WET PAINT BILL

Anybody need their umbrella fixed? Oh, see here, Glue Needle,
some folks is out here in the street today. My, my, you all exercise
while you runnin' away or are you playin' "tick-a-tag"?
. . . "catch-a-baby"? Now that's a fine game.

OLD GLUE NEEDLE

Uh-hmm. (*with a pointed glance at the Electric Piggybank Man*)
Do you ever play "pig in the blanket"?

WET PAINT BILL

Or "poke the mule with the umbrella"? (*As the Oreo Cookie Man
replies, Dorothy Doughie sings "Swanee" and pantomimes
strumming a banjo. The Oreo Cookie Man plays this broadly, an
obvious caricature.*)

OREO COOKIE MAN

No, brother. No, we're just out here on the street today, sellin' our
recipes, brother. Gimme some skin. Ruby begonia. (*He extends
his hand to Wet Paint Bill, who just looks at him.*)

WET PAINT BILL

Uh, what you do, mister? Did you fall into the mud pen?

OREO COOKIE MAN

(*maintaining a fake smile*) Chitlins!

WET PAINT BILL

Look, Glue Needle, he fell into the muddy pen.

OREO COOKIE MAN

Corn pone!

WET PAINT BILL

Why, sir, you got yourself a dirty face.

OREO COOKIE MAN

White Cadillac!

WET PAINT BILL

Here, take my handkerchief and wipe that off! (*He pulls out a
handkerchief and wipes the Oreo Cookie Man's face, revealing
white skin. The Oreo Cookie Man panics.*)

OREO COOKIE MAN

Oh, no! (*He runs to the Dream Wagon and grabs a whiteface mask. He adopts a Chamber of Commerce manner.*) Very glad to meet you out here on the street today, sir. (*He turns to Daddy Tutti-Fruit Hat and they shake hands.*) All right, George, I'll bring the insurance policy by tomorrow.

DADDY TUTTI-FRUIT HAT

Thanks so much for stopping by, Jim. Say hello to the wife and kids. (*The Oreo Cookie Man steps behind Daddy Tutti-Fruit Hat and removes the mask.*)

WET PAINT BILL

You folks pardon us, we're just out in the street today doin' our work.

OLD GLUE NEEDLE

Some of you seem to be standin' around. I wonder if you have need of our expertise and skill.

WET PAINT BILL

Ten cents takes care of it, work guaranteed against hailstorm and lightning.

OLD GLUE NEEDLE

Unless you deserve it, and then of course you're goin' to get it anyway. (*The sound of thunder is produced on the percussion.*)

WET PAINT BILL

We'd be pleased to help you out.

STALE CAKE COMPANY

(*chanting*) Well! What! Do! You! Do! (*Theme: "Old Glue Needle and Wet Paint Bill." * Old Glue Needle and Wet Paint Bill sing the first part a cappella.*)

OLD GLUE NEEDLE

Umbrellas . . .

WET PAINT BILL

Umbrellas . . .

(*The members of the Stale Cake Company cower around the ladder.*)

*Music on page 302.

OLD GLUE NEEDLE and WET PAINT BILL

>*Umbrellas repaired, parasols mended,*
>*Let us take you back to where the Lord intended.*

(*The orchestra picks up the song. The two men dance a gentle, old-fashioned vaudeville soft-shoe routine.*)

>*He's Old Glue Needle and I'm Wet Paint Bill.*
>*If you need anything mended,*
>*Just ask us and we will*
>*Be glad to do with a stitch and a dab,*
>*But you better let us fix you*
>*Before it gets too bad.*

>*Umbrellas repaired, parasols mended,*
>*Let us get you back to where the Lord intended.*
>*Umbrellas repaired, ten pennies if you will . . .*

OLD GLUE NEEDLE

>*Done by Old Glue Needle . . .*

WET PAINT BILL

>*. . . and Wet Paint Bill.*

(*They sing the melody on "doo" as children enter, bringing umbrellas for repair. The children cross past the Stale Cake Company and out with repaired umbrellas. The members of the Stale Cake Company try to entice them, but the children ignore them.*)

OLD GLUE NEEDLE and WET PAINT BILL

>*If the rain's coming in and you're catching cold,*
>*There's a good medicine, so I been told:*
>*Go down to the meadow*
>*In the full moonlight*
>*And say hello to the Lord—*
>*Now you be polite.*

>*He'll give you your share,*
>*That's as he intended.*
>*So hurry on, mister, get your canvas mended.*
>*Umbrellas repaired, hope our work pleases you,*

But if you wanta get fixed quick
Put on your dancin' shoes.
(*They continue the dance routine, making remarks to each other*
as they dance.)

OLD GLUE NEEDLE

How ya doin', Bill?

WET PAINT BILL

Oh, tolerable! (*Old Glue Needle sits on Wet Paint Bill's lap.*)

OLD GLUE NEEDLE

A puppet! I want something now, Mama! . . . Get in the boat,
Bill! Lewis and Clark! (*They pretend to row a boat.*)

WET PAINT BILL

Oh, explorers! (*Old Glue Needle stands in front of the Stale Cake*
Company as Wet Paint Bill poses on one foot, his hand over his
eyes as if looking far into the distance. Wet Paint Bill looks
toward the audience as Old Glue Needle stares at the Stale Cake
Company.)

OLD GLUE NEEDLE

It's still there, Bill.

WET PAINT BILL

Oh, it is?

OLD GLUE NEEDLE

Why, didn't you think it would be?

WET PAINT BILL

I thought it would be, but I don't think it should be . . . (*They*
turn and walk upstage with tiny, mincing steps.)

OLD GLUE NEEDLE

Tiny steps.

WET PAINT BILL

Minuscule. (*They put their umbrellas behind their heads and lean*
back on them as if against pillows.)

OLD GLUE NEEDLE

Bedtime. (*He pretends to row a boat; Wet Paint Bill climbs into*
the boat and helps row.) Let's go . . . England!

WET PAINT BILL

France!

OLD GLUE NEEDLE

    Germany!

WET PAINT BILL

    All by boat!

OLD GLUE NEEDLE

    Kansas!

OLD GLUE NEEDLE and WET PAINT BILL

    (*singing*)

> *So remember, my friends,*
> *We hope you take it to heart,*
> *When the old world looks confused*
> *And your mind is comin' apart,*
> *Take a dab from Old Glue Needle*
> *And a stitch from Wet Paint Bill,*
> *Fix the tears in your umbrella,*
> *Let us paint your windowsill.*
> *Get the life that's good and simple,*
> *It's not easy but you try,*
> *Find a message for your neighbor,*
> *He will read it by and by . . .*

DADDY TUTTI-FRUIT HAT

    (*writing everything down in a tiny notebook, mumbling to himself*) "He will read it by and by."

OLD GLUE NEEDLE and WET PAINT BILL

    (*singing*)

> *You'll hurry to the meadow*
> *Where the water's runnin' still . . .*

WET PAINT BILL

    (*speaking over his shoulder to the Oreo Cookie Man*) If you don't get that face cleaned up, you never goin' to make it! (*The Oreo Cookie Man growls at him.*)

OLD GLUE NEEDLE and WET PAINT BILL

    (*singing*)

> *Where you'll meet Old Glue Needle*
> *And Wet Paint Bill.*

    (*By the end of the song they are seated on the repair wagon.*)

DADDY TUTTI-FRUIT HAT

Well, well, that's all well and good, fellas. I mean I digga dig, I dig your spiel, I dig your schtick, but nobody uses umbrellas any more these days . . . We've got everything you kids could possibly want or need. Whatta ya need, huh?

BLACK-EYED PEA

Could you fix my umbrella?

DADDY TUTTI-FRUIT HAT

(*confidently*) Could we fix your umbrella! (*to the Stale Cake Company*) Could we fix her umbrella? (*to Black-Eyed Pea*) Why, sure, honey, give it here . . . (*He grabs her umbrella and the Stale Cake Company huddles, growling and thrashing. Daddy Tutti-Fruit Hat emerges from the huddle with Dorothy Doughie's spoon. He takes it to Black-Eyed Pea.*) A Dorothy Doughie! (*Black-Eyed Pea looks at it in disgust.*)

BLACK-EYED PEA

Could I have my umbrella back?

DADDY TUTTI-FRUIT HAT

Whatta ya mean? Put it over your head . . . (*He swings the spoon over his head, demonstrating.*)

OREO COOKIE MAN

Oh, that's a dandy, that's a dandy! (*Daddy Tutti-Fruit Hat sees that Black-Eyed Pea is not interested, and he strides back to the group. Again they jam together, growling, and Daddy Tutti-Fruit Hat emerges with Diana Dumbstrut's giant eggbeater.*)

DADDY TUTTI-FRUIT HAT

A Diana Dumbstrut '72 model! Chrome reverse wheels, candy apple red . . . put it right over your head and turn it real fast . . . (*He demonstrates.*)

DIANA DUMBSTRUT

It's just like hers! (*Black-Eyed Pea shakes her head. Daddy Tutti-Fruit Hat returns to the group and emerges with Black-Eyed Pea's parasol.*)

DADDY TUTTI-FRUIT HAT

Here! (*He gives the parasol back to her.*)

OLD GLUE NEEDLE

She's got you whipped, Mister Fruit Hat.

DADDY TUTTI-FRUIT HAT

I know what you people need! A little bit of Stale Cake! I want each and every one of you to take one of these individually cellophane-wrapped packages of Stale Cake . . . from Daddy Tutti-Fruit Hat, with love. (*The members of the Stale Cake Company say "Mmmmm!" lick their lips, and pat their tummies. They croon the theme song off-key as Daddy Tutti-Fruit Hat takes pieces of cake wrapped in cellophane from the Dream Wagon and gives them to Wet Paint Bill, Old Glue Needle, and the children. They bite into the cake, but obviously it is no taste treat.*)

OLD GLUE NEEDLE

Well, we're sorry to say this, but . . .

WET PAINT BILL

This cake . . .

BUBBLE

This cake . . .

BLACK-EYED PEA

. . . is stale!

WET PAINT BILL

You should come to our house sometime. We got *good* cake.

OLD GLUE NEEDLE

You could put a cover over it and keep it moist.

BUBBLE

You need a recipe for this stuff?

BLACK-EYED PEA

Pardon me, Miss Doughie, maybe your bowl is a little on the dirty side of things.

DADDY TUTTI-FRUIT HAT

All right! We've got your number, sweetheart! (*The members of the Stale Cake Company glower at the men and the children and exit in a huff.*)

OLD GLUE NEEDLE

We'll see you, Mister Fruit Hat!

WET PAINT BILL

My, my, never tasted the stuff they were passin' out.

OLD GLUE NEEDLE

That's like sellin' vinegar for water 'cause it comes in a bottle.

WET PAINT BILL

(*to Bubble and Black-Eyed Pea*) Say, you want to join us in a song?

BUBBLE and BLACK-EYED PEA

Yeah!

OLD GLUE NEEDLE

OK. One, two, three . . . (*Reprise: "Old Glue Needle and Wet Paint Bill."** *They all sing on "doo," pretending to play musical instruments, parading with umbrellas, and marching upstage. Upstage, they turn to sing to the audience.*)

ALL

> *Get the life that's good and simple,*
> *It's not easy but you try,*
> *Find a message for your neighbor,*
> *He will read it by and by . . .*

(*Thunder. They open their umbrellas, holding them like parasols behind them.*)

> *You'll hurry to the meadow*
> *Where the water's runnin' still,*
> *There you'll meet Old Glue Needle*
> *And Wet Paint Bill.*

(*They close their umbrellas and dance out as the lights cross-fade and the Matchbox House slides into place.*)

---

*Music on page 302.

Scene vii   Mother Mary
and the Matchbox House

Bubble, Black-Eyed Pea, Wet Paint Bill, and Old Glue Needle slide in, greeting Mother Mary and laughing. Mother Mary, seated in an armchair, is painting at an easel.

MOTHER MARY

Hi! I'm just paintin' up this picture of the sun. Ain't this nice? I've been learning how to draw and paint with the kids these days. But I got up this morning and sat out on the step in the yard and painted this picture of the sun sitting in the sky. Don't that make a picture, though? Hurry up, Bill, lemonade needs squeezin' before the cookies get cold. Needle, get the glasses out, if you please. Oh, my! Who's this? Well, guests in the Matchbox! How do you do? (*Bubble and Black-Eyed Pea go to her and sit on the arms of her chair.*)

BUBBLE and BLACK-EYED PEA

Hello, ma'am.

MOTHER MARY

What's your name?

BLACK-EYED PEA

Black-Eyed Pea.

BUBBLE

Bubble.

MOTHER MARY

Well, I'm Mother Mary, the cook. How do you do? Tell me, how did you two get here? Nobody don't come to this place unless they come with Needle and Bill. What you gotta say?

BUBBLE

Bill and Glue Needle helped us from some trouble.

MOTHER MARY

Oh yeah, what's the matter?

260

BLACK-EYED PEA

Well, these people were trying to chase us and stuff.

WET PAINT BILL

Chase ya? They'd like to turn you into butter.

OLD GLUE NEEDLE

They looked to me like they were picking after strawberries.

MOTHER MARY

Well, what were ya doing to get yourself chased around the street on a hot day like this?

BUBBLE

Well, they wanted us to buy something.

MOTHER MARY

Buy what?

BLACK-EYED PEA

Oh, all kinds of stuff nobody needed.

BUBBLE

We didn't need it.

MOTHER MARY

Like what?

BLACK-EYED PEA

Oh, some portable something or other. You're supposed to put it on your head. It's got lights, plays music, and cooks up some toasted waffle or something.

BUBBLE

Yeah, and tells you the time.

BLACK-EYED PEA

Yeah, and glows in the dark.

BUBBLE

Yeah, and smells like pine needles when you squeeze it.

OLD GLUE NEEDLE

And has a heater in it.

WET PAINT BILL

And it can be used as a can opener for sardines, oh my!

MOTHER MARY

Ah me, oh my! Does it take your shoes off, too, and rub your tired old feet? I wonder if it knows how to squeeze lemonade and do the washing! If it can, I just might get myself a couple of them things and tell these old two to get on. (*She laughs.*) But what you two do to get them sellin' folks to chase you around the place?

BUBBLE

Nothing. Just asked them if they knew how to skip stones.

MOTHER MARY

What'd they say?

BUBBLE

No.

BLACK-EYED PEA

Uh-huh.

MOTHER MARY

What else?

BLACK-EYED PEA

Oh, and if they could bake bread.

MOTHER MARY

What'd they say?

BUBBLE

No.

BLACK-EYED PEA

And if they had black-eyed pea seeds.

MOTHER MARY

What'd they say?

BUBBLE and BLACK-EYED PEA

No!

MOTHER MARY

(*turning to Wet Paint Bill and Old Glue Needle*) And what'd you two say?

WET PAINT BILL

Oh, nothin'!

OLD GLUE NEEDLE

Just asked them if they could mend an umbrella.

MOTHER MARY

Oh, oh.

BUBBLE and BLACK-EYED PEA

And they said no.

MOTHER MARY

Oh! What kind of people can't even patch up an old umbrella?

WET PAINT BILL

Most kinds, I expect, these days. Most folks just throw away everything that's gettin' the least bit old and buy something new.

OLD GLUE NEEDLE

They don't fix nothin', Mary.

WET PAINT BILL

They don't care to preserve nothin' old, nothin' that's been good to them for years. Instead they're looking for something new.

OLD GLUE NEEDLE

And shiny. New and shiny. Well, I saw an umbrella the other day that didn't even look like one. The only way I could tell the fella thought that's what it was, was it started to rain and he stuck the damn thing over his head. I'll show you what it looked like. (*He goes to the easel and begins to paint a picture of the umbrella.*) It had a window here and another one here and a third window here, and it had a fourth window right here in the center. Looked more like a decorated rocket ship with windows to me. Been better off with a garbage can cover.

WET PAINT BILL

I'd have to make up something to do with most of the stuff they had to sell. Why, they had one thing they called a ramma-stramma . . .

OLD GLUE NEEDLE

Here, now, watch your language in front of the kids. Mary, it seems to me that most folks today ain't even heard of a glass of plain water.

WET PAINT BILL

They looked like they'd never heard of plain old people.

BUBBLE

There wasn't one thing they had that I wanted.

BLACK-EYED PEA

Me neither.

MOTHER MARY

Why, what did those folks go by? What name?

BUBBLE

The Stale Cake Company. (*They laugh.*)

MOTHER MARY

Well, now that figures. There ain't nothin' to do with a hunk of stale cake, 'cept nothin'.

BUBBLE

Yeah, but they were giving away lots of pieces of that cake, and all the kids were taking it and cheering and shouting "Wa-hoo!" and puttin' it in their shopping bags.

BLACK-EYED PEA

Yeah, and paying Big Money for all their stuff.

BUBBLE

Some of them got some really shiny stuff to take home. Maybe we should try it.

BLACK-EYED PEA

Don't you say it. You want to turn into a pig or somethin', boy?

WET PAINT BILL

They had this one man — looked just like a pig.

OLD GLUE NEEDLE

They had this one *pig* that looked just like a *man.*

WET PAINT BILL

Oink, oink . . . Here's the lemonade and here's the cookies. Hot and fresh. (*Wet Paint Bill and Old Glue Needle make a production out of serving the food. They sing a fanfare, "ta-tata-ta-tata," and march to the children and Mary, carrying the food and singing.*)

WET PAINT BILL and OLD GLUE NEEDLE

Oh, the Stale Cake
Is the real cake!

WET PAINT BILL

That's just how the Stale Cake song went. OK, now. Everybody take one of these. You're gonna get a chance now to try a special old recipe of mine. A long time ago this was given to me by my mother. She said to me, "Bill, one of these days, you're gonna be on your own and you're gonna get a chance to make this yourself.

Then you can give it to somebody and have them taste it." This is
old, Mother Mary, now tell me what it's like.

MOTHER MARY

Well, Bill, it tastes old (*they laugh*) . . . but it's delicious.

BUBBLE

Wow! These are the best cookies I ever tasted!

BLACK-EYED PEA

Uh-huh!

MOTHER MARY

You think so? Tell 'em, you two.

OLD GLUE NEEDLE

Well, you see, not everybody thinks these here cookies are the best
they've ever tasted.

BUBBLE

Why? They're terrific.

BLACK-EYED PEA

Really!

WET PAINT BILL

That's right. But not everybody likes the same things.

OLD GLUE NEEDLE

Now, you know and I know Mother Mary's cookies are the best.

WET PAINT BILL

I know so many people that think that other cookies are better.

OLD GLUE NEEDLE

Just like those people that were eating away on that stale
cake.

WET PAINT BILL

And if you don't know what's good in the first place, how you
gonna tell the difference when you see it?

MOTHER MARY, OLD GLUE NEEDLE, and WET PAINT BILL

When it's lookin' ya in the face.

MOTHER MARY

No sir, you gotta know to taste my sugar and spice. And that ain't
easy for some folks. Now, you two, you like to sit up in a tree?
And you, out on the roof?

BLACK-EYED PEA and BUBBLE
> Yeah.

MOTHER MARY
> Fresh water?

BLACK-EYED PEA
> Yeah.

MOTHER MARY
> And the wind and singing?

BLACK-EYED PEA and BUBBLE
> Yeah.

MOTHER MARY
> And quiet times in the back patch?

BLACK-EYED PEA and BUBBLE
> Yeah.

MOTHER MARY
> So maybe your old nose is just in fine shape to taste a cookie and know it's settin' fine. But don't you think, babies, that everybody sees it, 'cause there's plenty of people out there wantin' a portable whatever-it-is, just to make them feel happy. Amen to that.

ALL
> Amen.

MOTHER MARY
> But anyway, we know what we like and we're doing it. Ain't we? Let's enjoy it.

ALL
> Yeah! (*They applaud and ad-lib as they eat and drink during Winde's entrance. Winde is dressed as a grocery store worker, and he carries a bag of groceries.*)

WINDE
> Groceries!

MOTHER MARY
> OK, honey, put 'em back there anywhere. Thank you. (*Old Glue Needle brings out an ironing board covered with a lace cloth; a piano keyboard rests on the board. He puts it in front of Mother Mary.*) Here's one of my favorite things. Bubble, Black-Eyed Pea, come over here. Bill and Needle, come over here and gather

round. I never did find room for a piano in here 'cause it's so small here in this Matchbox. But I got Needle to pull this here old keyboard in here. Now I'm just fine. It's kind of magic. I just push on the keys and out comes the music. (*She "plays" on the keyboard, and a piano is heard playing "Sweet Jesus, Precious Savior."**)

BUBBLE

I don't hear it.

MOTHER MARY

That's what I mean, baby. That's like the cookie: Ya can't taste it 'til ya taste it, and with this old thing ya can't hear it 'til ya hear it. But when you do hear it, honey, you HEAR it! And we're hearin' it just fine. Right, you two?

WET PAINT BILL and OLD GLUE NEEDLE

Right! (*Mother Mary plays on the keyboard again, and a few more measures of the song are heard.*)

BUBBLE

Let me try!

MOTHER MARY

OK. Come on. (*Bubble sits at the keyboard and tries to play, but nothing happens.*)

BUBBLE

I just don't hear it.

MOTHER MARY

Try it now, right there. (*She takes Bubble's finger and places it on the keyboard. As she does so, each of the men places a hand on one of Bubble's shoulders. This time a few measures of the song are heard.*)

BUBBLE

Wow! It works!

MOTHER MARY

Of course.

OLD GLUE NEEDLE

Really!

*Music on page 300.

WET PAINT BILL

Don't say. (*Mother Mary, Black-Eyed Pea, and the cast sing "Sweet Jesus, Precious Savior."*)

MOTHER MARY

Lead me home,
Lead me home, now,
Sweet, sweet Jesus!
O-o-oh!

(*The members of the cast take positions at the back of the auditorium, in the balcony, and in the wings to sing "oooh!" as an accompaniment to the solo lines.*)

Through the storm,
Through the night,
Lead me home!

BLACK-EYED PEA

I am tired,
I am weary,
And the world grows
Cold around me.
Precious Jesus,
Precious Savior,
Lead me home!

BLACK-EYED PEA	CAST
Lead me home . . .	*Lead me home now!*
Lead me home . . .	*Lead me home now!*
Lead me home . . .	*Lead me home now!*
Lead me home through	
the night . . .	*Lead me home . . .*
Through the storm . . .	*Lead me home!*
Lead me home!	

ALL

Oh Lord, lead me home!

BLACK-EYED PEA	CAST
I am tired . . .	*Lead me home!*
I am weary . . .	*Lead me home!*
And the world grows . . .	*Lead me home!*
Cold around me . . .	*Lead me home!*

ALL

> *Precious Jesus*
> *Precious Savior,*
> *Lead me home!*

(*Black-Eyed Pea and Bubble run out, waving and saying good-bye to Mother Mary, Winde, Wet Paint Bill, and Old Glue Needle, who remain at the keyboard singing. The lights fade down. The Matchbox House slides offstage.*)

Scene viii   "Get, Get, Get!"

Winde addresses the audience from a pool of light.

WINDE

Very nice. There's a real nice breeze blowin' through that Matchbox House . . . Just what a body needs to feel right — a little nudge from the spirit on a warm day . . . but on the other hand, I feel the wind coming down the other direction with just more than a little smell of something rotten in it. Smells to me like a piece of stale cake. I don't believe that everybody that bought a recipe today was exactly filled with smiles for his fellow man. You know how it is — when somebody gets something new that's his alone and his only, he doesn't want to share it with his neighbor . . . Yup, I think I detect the smell of burnt cake drifting by my nose . . . What do you think? (*Boogie lead-in to "Get, Get, Get!" Ricky and Ronn stride in from the right and left wings and hostilely confront each other. Winde exits.*)

RONN

Oh!

RICKY

Yeah!

RONN

No!

RICKY

Huh!

RONN

Huh!

RICKY

Huh! (*Black-Eyed Pea and Bubble enter and greet the two boys.*)

BUBBLE

Hi!

RONN

Get out of here! (*Black-Eyed Pea and Bubble run out.*)

RICKY

Go on! Mine is!

RONN

No! Mine is!

RICKY

We'll see, we'll see!

RONN

We'll see nothin'!

RICKY

See this! (*He punches Ronn in the eye. Theme: "The Stale Cake Company," march tempo. Dorothy Doughie enters, sees the conflict, and blows her whistle for the Electric Piggybank Man and the Dream Wagon to enter.*)

DOROTHY DOUGHIE

(*sweetly*) What's the matter, boys? Did you have an argument?

RONN

The recipe I bought from the Stale Cake is best! And I'll prove it!

DOROTHY DOUGHIE

(*again sweetly*) Oohhh! You're right! Well then, here. (*speaking in a gang moll's aside to Ronn*) Buy now, pay later! (*She gets a wooden saber from the Dream Wagon and hands it to Ronn, hiding it from Ricky.*)

RICKY

No, no, no! Mine's the best and I'll prove it!

DOROTHY DOUGHIE

(*sweetly*) Oohhh! I'm sure it is. (*speaking again as a gang moll, this time to Ricky*) Today, for you, a discount. (*She gives him a saber also, hiding it from Ronn. She sings to the tune of "Good Ship Lollipop."*)

    On the good ship Kill a Lot . . .

(*She giggles and runs off with the Electric Piggybank Man and the Dream Wagon. Ronn and Ricky begin to fight. Sheila and Maureen push between them to the center of the stage.*)

SHEILA

(*chanting as she reads from a recipe*) Take two cups of lever and two cups of jever. Wait 'til it's hard and it's good forever!

MAUREEN

Oh yeah! That's nothin'! Wait until you see the size of mine. Besides, mine has an elevator in it! (*A guitar makes a musical comment. Maureen speaks to the guitarist.*) Hey! That's pretty good, man.

SHEILA

Oh yeah!

MAUREEN

Yeah! And when I'm the head one, you're goin' to be the end one!

RICKY

Same for you, too! (*A battle ensues with Ronn fighting Ricky and Sheila fighting Maureen. Captain Steal enters.*)

CAPTAIN STEAL

Aye, maties! Aye, maties! Only ladies and gents! Please! Here, try one of these!

CHILDREN

Wow! Far out!

CAPTAIN STEAL

This is the Super Ding-A-Ling Buzz Ball! (*He pulls out a grenade device.*) Spreads all sorts of disease! (*chanting*) With one of these, you can smash in their heads! Get one of these, you can knock them all dead.

CHILDREN

I'll take one of those! I'll take ten of those, from you! Where's mine?

ELECTRIC PIGGYBANK MAN

> Good kids! That's only $14.92!

CAPTAIN STEAL

> Here, try a case! (*The battle resumes. The members of the Stale Cake Company weave among the children, yelling and selling weapons. Underscore: lead-in to "Get, Get, Get!"*)

ELECTRIC PIGGYBANK MAN

> Weapons for war! Weapons for war! Programs for the war!

CLINTON

> (*chanting*) Now everybody, I mean everybody, just listen to me! 'Cause, baby, I plan on takin' over with my recipe. So everybody just cool back and settle down, 'cause I'm takin' over in this town!

ARTIE and CYN

> (*taking turns chanting phrases*) One cup of flabbers, one cup of gebats. Man, when we get done with this, it's going to be bad! Right on!

CLINTON

> Bad! You mean sad!

BRIDGET

> Yours stinks!

ARTIE

> You're finks!

CYN

> (*chanting*) This is a Dobas Franges Fretter, and there can be nothing better, and if you guys don't believe us, you'd better leave us! (*Some of the children throw grenades at others. Another fight begins.*)

KIM

> (*singing*) The Stale Cake is the real cake! (*chanting*) And I'm the one that's going to do the big bake that's going to break me into the lead! Here's all I need! Can you believe it? Well, you can see it! And pretty soon, you're all goin' to eat it!

OREO COOKIE MAN

> Right on, soul sister! You heard it from Mr. Oreo! (*All perform a minstrel routine of hand-clapping and seat-slapping as "Swanee" is played on the piano, underscoring the Oreo Cookie Man's*

speech. He begins to chant.) Hello, I see you're on the go. But you've gotta have your flapper gun, you know! Here's your crown, go to town, just waitin' for you to gun 'em down! (*Kim starts to take a toy bazooka from him.*) That'll be $6.97, honey! (*She pays him with Big Money and then pretends to shoot everyone with the gun. A percussion instrument sounds the shots.*)

STEVEN

(*chanting in rhythm with the music*) Keeno! Neato! I repeato! I just won the championship with my recipe for a sailing ship! I'll take the lead 'cause I got the speed to do the deed! You guys are creeps! Yes, I repeat, you guys are creeps! Your stuff is cheap! (*speaking conversationally*) Why don't you take a leap into a dirty dish pan! I am the man! (*All attack Steven. Diana Dumbstrut leads the Stale Cake Company and the children in a yell.*)

ALL

Fight, fight, fight! Kill, kill, kill! Fight, fight, fight, fight, you're a pill! Yay! War! (*All fight and dance. Jenny enters with a megaphone. They all chant.*) Mine's the best, mine's the best, everybody knows that mine's the best!

DEBBIE

(*chanting*) Fiddy biddy bye, fiddy biddy bo, you're a little too smart so you've got to go! (*She knocks Jenny to the ground.*)

ALL

Yay! (*The following lines are chanted.*)

DIANA DUMBSTRUT

So take your own!

CAPTAIN STEAL

Take it home!

DOROTHY DOUGHIE

But you've gotta make sure that you're all alone!

OREO COOKIE MAN

Don't let anybody touch it, remember that!

ELECTRIC PIGGYBANK MAN

Keep all the good stuff under your hat!

DADDY TUTTI-FRUIT HAT

Remember . . . Stale Cake, Stale Cake, S-T-A-L-E . . . Stale Cake!

ALL

(*repeating about six times*) Stale Cake! Stale Cake! Stale Cake! Stale Cake! Stale Cake! Stale Cake! (*Piano theme: "Sweet Jesus, Precious Savior." Black-Eyed Pea and Bubble enter with lemonade and cookies for all.*)

BLACK-EYED PEA

Hi, you guys, want some lemonade? It's fresh and just squeezed and made of fresh real lemons.

BUBBLE

And fresh cookies, too, still hot.

RONN

Gimme one of those cookies. I'll pay five. How much are they?

MAUREEN

I'll take a dozen. I've got plenty of money. And put it on my elevator.

AUDREY

Give me some lemonade.

ARTIE

Don't give her nothin'. She ain't got no money. I got most of it.

SHEILA

Give me lots of those cookies, I've got Big Money. (*A melee erupts with everyone yelling and grabbing.*)

BLACK-EYED PEA

You don't need money, we've got plenty. They're free.

BUBBLE

Yes. See?

CAPTAIN STEAL

You don't give nothin' away!

ELECTRIC PIGGYBANK MAN

If you got somethin' somebody wants, you make 'em pay.

DIANA DUMBSTRUT

(*leading them in a cheer*) Say "pay"!

ALL

>Pay!

DIANA DUMBSTRUT

>Say "yay"!

ALL

>Yay!

BLACK-EYED PEA

>Why pay when everything's free . . .

BUBBLE

>And good . . .

BLACK-EYED PEA

>Today! (*Theme: "Get, Get, Get!"* Daddy Tutti-Fruit Hat whips everyone but Bubble and Black-Eyed Pea into place.*)

DADDY TUTTI-FRUIT HAT

>(*speaking in rhythm*) We won't be underbid, my friends, so listen to our story. The best buy in a recipe will make you . . .

DIANA DUMBSTRUT and WOMEN

>(*singing*)

>>. . . *rich before you're forty!*

DADDY TUTTI-FRUIT HAT

>And now, here to tell you more is Captain Steal! (*The girls squeal. Ginni crawls to Captain Steal and hugs his leg.*)

GINNI

>I love you, Captain Steal!

CAPTAIN STEAL

>I love you, too, Cookie. (*He recites the verse in rhythm. The cast sings "bum-bum" in tempo in the background.*)

>>*So assemble all your stuff, my friends,*
>>*Your bricks, your gold, and your booty,*
>>*And be sure and buy our recipes*
>>*'Cause if you don't, you will be sorry!*

ALL

>(*singing*)

>>*Ya gotta get, get, get!*
>>*Ya gotta get, get, get!*

*Music on page 303.

> *If the world's in trouble*
> *And you don't know what to do,*
> *Ya gotta get, get, get!*
> *Hey hey, hey ho!*
> *Hey hey, hey ho!*

DADDY TUTTI-FRUIT HAT

Now, here comes the Oreo Cookie Man! (*The cast continues to sing "hey hey, hey ho" under the Oreo Cookie Man's speech.*)

OREO COOKIE MAN

Brothers and sisters, brothers and sisters, yeah, yeah, yeah, yeah! (*He recites in rhythm.*)

> *Come here to me!*
> *Come here to me!*
> *Come look me in the eye.*
> *I'll make you rich,*
> *I'll make you happy,*
> *If you'll only let me try!*

(*He leaps back into the group; they sing "bum-bum" in the background as Daddy Tutti-Fruit Hat comes forward again.*)

DADDY TUTTI-FRUIT HAT

And now, Miss Diana Dumbstrut, the Girl with the Golden Goose! Tell 'em, Diana! (*Diana Dumbstrut struts to him.*)

DIANA DUMBSTRUT

First you need a suit! And some shiny boots! And a diamond cookie cutter! (*She blows her whistle and does a backbend. Then she marches in place furiously as the music bursts briefly into a Sousa march and everyone cheers. Then the group resumes the "bum-bum" background.*)

DADDY TUTTI-FRUIT HAT

And now, for the first time in public, the Stale Cake Company's very own Franges Dober Flutter! Only $11.95 at toy department stores everywhere . . . (*speaking rapidly through "included"*) requires-seven-Eveready- Triple- A- Penlight- batteries- batteries- not-included . . . Because I am Daddy Tutti-Fruit Hat and I stand behind each and every one of my Stale Cake Company products, I'm going to be the first to try on the Franges Dober

Flutter. (*He has been putting the gadget on his head as he speaks.*)
Go ahead! (*to one of the crowd*) Turn that thing! (*Everyone
shrieks. The lights go down and the Franges Dober Flutter lights
up. Daddy Tutti-Fruit Hat does a frantic shimmy dance, jumping
up and down in the darkness with the glowing Franges Dober
Flutter on his head. It vaguely resembles a modernistic lamp with
filaments that "spray" out from the' base. A burst of music
accompanies this brief display. The Franges Dober Flutter
music ends and the vamp resumes.*) A little bit much for Daddy
Tutti-Fruit Hat! (*He gives the Franges Dober Flutter to the
Electric Piggybank Man and retrieves the Fruit Hat.*) And now
here she is, the world's favorite cream puff, Miss Dorothy
Doughie!

DOROTHY DOUGHIE

(*singing and dancing in place*)
> You need a pile of flops
> And a box of drops
> And a luster-crusted fretter
> And a golden chain of Stink-o-Lets . . .

(*The members of the cast bounce and sway from side to side as
they sing the following lyrics.*)

ALI

> *Who-o-o!*

MEN

> *Nothing could be better!*

ALL

> *Ya gotta get, get, get!*
> *Ya gotta get, get, get!*

WOMEN

> *Oh, you'll never be happy . . .*

MEN

> *. . . get rich very quick*
> *Unless you get, get, get!*

DADDY TUTTI-FRUIT HAT

Now here comes . . . (*the girls squeal*) Captain Steal! (*Ginni
runs to Captain Steal and clings to his leg.*) What's that,
sweetheart?

GINNI

  I love Captain Steal!

DADDY TUTTI-FRUIT HAT

  Far out! How old are you, darling?

GINNI

  Seven.

DADDY TUTTI-FRUIT HAT

  Seven. How old are you, Captain Steal? (*Captain Steal lowers his sunglasses and leers.*)

CAPTAIN STEAL

  Uh . . . thirteen! (*Squeals. The crowd sings "gotta get, gotta get, gotta get, get" as background for Captain Steal's lines. He recites in rhythm.*)

    So step aside, little lady . . .

  (*He kicks Ginni away.*)

    And witness this.

    It's a miracle of invention . . .

  (*He shows a gadget resembling a toothbrush with coils and wires.*)

    For to make you the queen
    With the streamlined gleam
    Is this machine's
    Intention!

  (*He steps aside.*)

DADDY TUTTI-FRUIT HAT

  (*in rhythm*) Try . . . that . . . machine. Now here comes a Stale Cake Company duet!

DIANA DUMBSTRUT and ELECTRIC PIGGYBANK MAN

  (*singing*)

    Be sure to do your homework,
    Check your list of don'ts and do's . . .

ALL

    Who-o-o!

  (*The crowd resumes the "gotta get" background. Through the rest of this scene there is no recitation; everything is sung.*)

DADDY TUTTI-FRUIT HAT

    When you get through

With our products,
You'll be the Girl
With the Golden Goose!

ALL

Ya gotta get, get, get!
Ya gotta get, get, get!
You'll never be the Train
With the Silver Caboose
Unless you get, get, get!
Buy, buy, assemble or you die!
Yes, get, get, get!

(*The dance begins in earnest. Ideally, the very walls would dance, spoons and chairs would sway, chandeliers would bob. All objects would become animate, swelling, bobbing, and dancing as if borrowed from a Betty Boop cartoon. Various colors of light bathe the dancers, who perform in the style of the gaudiest television spectaculars.*)

BASS VOICES

Get, get, get, get! Ya gotta get, get, get, get!
Ya gotta get, get, get, get! Ya gotta get, get, get!

(*The bass voices continue to sing as the altos join them.*)

ALTO VOICES

Hey hey, hey ho! Hey hey, hey ho!

(*A whistle is blown. The tenors join the altos.*)

TENOR VOICES

Gotta get, gotta get, gotta get, get!
Gotta get, gotta get, gotta get, get!
Gotta get, gotta get, gotta get, get!
Gotta get, gotta get, gotta get, get!

(*A dance sequence with no lyrics begins and lasts for several minutes. The entire cast takes part in the dance. Shifting colored floodlights illuminate the stage and contribute to the motion and activity of the dance. As the dance sequence ends, the cast resumes the lyrics. Dorothy Doughie dances and sings a solo pseudo-jazz counterpoint to the music at a point indicated in the score.*)

ALL

DOROTHY DOUGHIE

Get, get, get, get!

Shi-poopie tittie
  ah-doo-da-pow!

Everybody's got to get!
Everybody's got to, got to
Get, get, get!

Chuck-full of moo-moo
And a poo-poo cow!
Noodle oodle doodle,
Sock-a-whammie doll,
Money, money,
  and a checkbook!

WOMEN

Got to, got to, got to, got to . . .

MEN

Get, get, get, get, get, get, get!

SOPRANO VOICES

ALTO VOICES

Gotta get . . .
Gotta get . . .
Gotta get . . .
Gotta get!

Got to . . .
Got to . . .
Got to . . .
Got to!

ALL

Get, get, get!

(*As the song continues, Dorothy Doughie sings and dances the counterpoint as the others sing and dance to the refrain. The effect is that of barely controlled chaos. Dorothy Doughie finishes in time to sing the final "get, get, get" with the others.*)

ALL

DOROTHY DOUGHIE

Get, get, get, get!
Everybody's got to get!
Everybody's got to get!
Ya gotta get!
Ya gotta get!
Ya gotta g-e-t!
Get, get, get, get, get!

Shi-pop-a-tutti-fruiti
Poodle and pie!
Hi-floogle-boogie-woogie
Pudding cup!

(*Smoke fills the stage. People are grabbing, chattering, and arguing. They scurry offstage. Daddy Tutti-Fruit Hat stands at the center, gleefully counting the Big Money. He whoops and runs off.*)

Scene ix   Famine

Winde steps through the smoke dressed as a fireman with yellow boots.

WINDE

Hmmm. Things seem to be getting a little hot around here. A bit smoky. A person could get burned. I got my yellow boots with the buckles, though, in case the floods come, too. Well, my friends, do you know what it's like to think that your house is the only little house on the block, that your new bike is the fastest, or your Dad's the smartest? Well now, if your little house catches on fire and your smartest Dad is trapped inside, and you're on your new red fastest bike just comin' home and you see it burning, you might have a hard time putting out the blaze without the help of a friend or two. I wonder if that ingredient is in your recipe. Add one cup of friends and blend thoroughly into a smooth mixture. Taste for sweetness. Let's look at a few recipes and see how folks are doin'. I'll watch and keep a record. You keep score. (*Winde sits on the rim of the bowl-world, where he is joined by Black-Eyed Pea, Wet Paint Bill, Old Glue Needle, and Bubble. Mother Mary leans against the proscenium. They observe the famine. Barry, Ricky, Steven, Holly, Bridget, and Artie bring out their recipes and gadgets. The children are scattered about the stage, each in his or her own world. All onstage speak and act at once. None of the recipes or devices work. The young people become increasingly frustrated, disgusted, and angry. A voiceover from an offstage microphone reverberates through the first part of the scene; the lines tumble upon one another and often are spoken simultaneously.*)

VOICEOVER

I'll be the King of TV! Get your Stale Cake Company King! Where's your queen crown, baby? Gotta get a king crown, gotta get a king-king, gotta get a king crown! A forty-piece orchestra,

your very own forty-piece orchestra, playing "Pomp and Circumstance." (*Falsetto voices hum "Pomp and Circumstance."*)
Jupiter and Mars! Venus, Pluto! Be the first kid on your block to
get to Jupiter! Stale Cake Company Space Kit! (*The voiceover
continues with similar lines from other points in the play. The
following speeches and actions overlap one another. Chaos.*)

RICKY

I'll be the King! I'm the TV star! Me and my forty-piece band!
When I'm the head one, you'll be the end one . . . maybe you'll
be no one! Shuffle to the TV star! (*He kicks his machine and it
falls apart.*) It does not work!

HOLLY

What's wrong, it doesn't work!

BRIDGET

Give me that! You've probably got mine.

HOLLY

Yours is probably mine! (*They try out their gadgets and nothing
works.*)

HOLLY and BRIDGET

These are wrong! They don't work!

BARRY

Wing-a-ding-ding! Just add one little thing! I am the King! I am
the King! (*He pantomimes putting on the King's clothes and gets
on his carpet.*) Where's the cheering? Where are the people?
Where's the coach? (*He adjusts his crown and tries again.*) My
subjects . . . where are the subjects? Where's the Queen? I am
the King! I am the King! I'm not the King.

STEVEN

I'll get to the moon! I'll get to Mars! Jupiter, here I come! Take
off! Take off! I'm not taking off! I'm not going anywhere! I'm not
taking off!

ARTIE

I'll be the star of the Ballet Cookie! Ballet Cookie of a Batch! Tie
on my little tutu! Russia, here I come! (*She puts on a tutu and
tries a ballet step. Parts of her costume fall off.*) I'm falling apart!
It doesn't work! I'm not the star of the Ballet Cookie! (*The

voiceover fades out. The children pick up their gadgets and devices and exit in tears as others move onto the stage. Theme: "Don't Be Grabbin' for More Than You've Got." Winde and his group begin to clap the rhythm of the song. The lights are dim. A hole near the floor is backlighted red, and the stage is smoky. The famine sequence is choreographed — people are struggling and stealing, weak with hunger: some are being pulled into the "hell hole." The clapping continues throughout the scene, and the Matchbox House group sings.)

WINDE

> *And the land was barren*
> *And nobody's recipe worked;*
> *People were at each other's throats,*
> *And all of the land went berserk.*

WINDE, BLACK-EYED PEA, MOTHER MARY, and WET PAINT BILL

> *Don't be grabbin' for more than you've got,*
> *Just know that you've got what you need.*
> *Don't be grabbin' for more than you've got,*
> *Just know that you've got what you need!*

MOTHER MARY

> *Folks were starvin'!*

BLACK-EYED PEA

> *Nobody knows what to do now!*

WINDE

> *Life's a sad state.*

WINDE, BLACK-EYED PEA, MOTHER MARY, and WET PAINT BILL

> *Taking from your neighbor*
> *And your good friends, too.*

ALL

> *Don't be grabbin' for more than you've got,*
> *Just know that you've got what you need!*
> *Don't be grabbin' for more than you've got,*
> *Just know that you've got what you need!*

WINDE

> *Then the rains came*
> *And the thunder broke.*

MOTHER MARY
> *And the Lord sent a wind through the land.*

MOTHER MARY and WET PAINT BILL
> *All the recipes for livin'*
> *Blew away to heaven . . .*

WINDE, BLACK-EYED PEA, MOTHER MARY, and WET PAINT BILL
> *. . . and the people had nowhere to turn.*

> *Don't be grabbin' for more than you've got,*
> *Just know that you've got what you need!*
> *Don't be grabbin' for more than you've got,*
> *Just know that you've got what you need!*

(*The chorus is repeated several times. Daddy Tutti-Fruit Hat appears as a silhouette in a shaft of smoky light, holding a bundle of money high while cracking his whip. He shouts "Money!" and the orchestra shouts back "Devil!" on the beats. Shouting, singing, and percussion build to a frenzy, then fade out as the lights go out. Winde continues to sing the chorus a cappella and changes into his "reporter" coat and hat as the Matchbox House is brought onstage in the darkness.*)

Scene x   State of
the Cookie Land Report

Winde is dressed as a newspaper reporter and carries a note pad and a pen. The Matchbox House is on the stage. Mother Mary, Wet Paint Bill, and Old Glue Needle sit in the Matchbox House listening to Winde.

WINDE
> Well, here I am, pickin' up the pieces, so to speak. State of the Cookie Land Report: The people of Cookie Land are on the

lookout for the Stale Cake Company, which was reported trying to leave town. It seems the people all purchased recipes for the Great Life, for which they paid all their Big Money. And it also seems that none of the recipes worked. And if the recipes did work, the people lost the directions on how to use them. Folks hereabout are very upset and are on the lookout for a sign or two. Meanwhile, the Stale Cake Company waits for the train to leave town. Bubble and Black-Eyed Pea left for Mother Mary's Matchbox. What to do? . . . Well . . . I'm just doing the reporting, not the fixing . . . It's a job for somebody . . . Well, maybe I will leave a small recipe. (*He smiles to himself and mumbles as he writes on his note pad.*) Let's see . . . toss some cake . . . (*He pins the note to the match that props up the rim of the bowl-world.*) See ya later, Bill!

WET PAINT BILL
Mmm-hmmm. (*He waves good-bye as Winde exits.*)

Scene xi   Mother Mary's Advice

Bubble and Black-Eyed Pea enter the Matchbox House on the slide, excited, their words tumbling out.

BUBBLE
Mother Mary, Mother Mary, things are terrible!

BLACK-EYED PEA
Yep. People are never goin' to make it. Everybody's all confused.

BUBBLE
Yeah! We don't know what to do!

BLACK-EYED PEA
What're we goin' to do?

MOTHER MARY
Well, I'm not goin' to say too much on the subject, kids, but if the

old lady forgot the recipe, or how to get things together, she should take a lesson from what she sees.

BLACK-EYED PEA

What do you mean? (*Lead-in to "Put It All Together into One Big Bowl!"**)

MOTHER MARY

(*singing*)

> Now you remember the words of a wise old bird;
> Oh, listen to the wisdom of a green bullfrog;
> Pay attention to the worms who stay up late at night;
> Put your ear down close to a log . . . you will always find
>   that . . .
>
> The bird in flight seeks other wings;
> The frog wants more singers on the lily pad.
> The little old worm likes company, oh yeah,
> Just look into a fisherman's can!

(*speaking*) You won't find just one worm there. No, lots of worms. Supposin' the ants are fixin' to build a pyramid . . . Do you think they'd attempt it divided . . . ? No! (*She continues to sing.*)

> So if it's raining and cold, with holes in your shoes,
> No marmalade, no pennies, no rent!

(*speaking*) And that's bad because they just come on out with the broom and sweep that homely sawdust lady out the door, you know? Uh-huh . . . (*She continues to sing.*)

> If there's ice on your nose and the wind blows froze
> Down your shirt, putting ice cubes down your back;
> If the worst comes to worst and you're ready to turn
> Into a stone from the bottom of some deep dark well . . .

(*speaking*) Well, remember the bird . . . the frog and the worm . . . What they *did*! And just think of the ant — almost forgot the little old ant . . . Just throw open your front door, even if it's winter, and call everybody into your home. Come on in, hurry now! Come now, woo hoo, hurry up, yoo hoo, get on in

*Music on pages 304 and 305.

here! And say . . . We're gonna put it all together in one big bowl! (*She continues to sing.*)

> Oh, put it all together into one big bowl;
> Mix a new batch of cookies, now you've been told!
> You'll never be hungry . . . in one big bowl;
> Put it all together into one big bowl!

(*speaking*) Now get on and do the invitin'. Tell 'em all, "Come on in here, 'cause we're gonna put it all together in one big bowl!" OK, hurry up now, invite 'em all in! (*The kids run out waving and calling "'Bye!" Wet Paint Bill and Old Glue Needle placidly strike the set as Mother Mary strolls out.*)

Scene xii   The Message

Black-Eyed Pea and Bubble wander across the stage disconsolately.

BLACK-EYED PEA

Have you thought of it?

BUBBLE

Huh-uuh! Did you?

BLACK-EYED PEA

No.

BUBBLE

Are you going to give up?

BLACK-EYED PEA

I don't know. Maybe. (*They think and lean on the match supporting the rim of the bowl-world. They do not see Winde's message.*) She said, "Put it all together in one big bowl," right?

BUBBLE

Yeah, but what was that about the bird and the ant?

BLACK-EYED PEA

(*musing*) Put it all together . . . into one big bowl.

BUBBLE

>(*seeing Winde's message*) Hey, what is this? A note . . . (*They read the message.*)

BLACK-EYED PEA

>It says, "Toss some cake . . ."

BUBBLE

>". . . and drop some money . . ."

BLACK-EYED PEA

>". . . If you stir just right . . ."

BUBBLE

>". . . things should turn into honey." (*They read the message again.*)

BLACK-EYED PEA

>Toss some cake, toss some cake . . .

BLACK-EYED PEA and BUBBLE

>*Stale* cake!

BUBBLE

>Money?

BLACK-EYED PEA

>Big Money!

BLACK-EYED PEA and BUBBLE

>Let's go! (*Boogie theme. Cymbals. Black-Eyed Pea and Bubble run offstage and return immediately with a bowl of Stale Cake pieces. They scatter the cake about, leaving a trail going offstage, and they exit hurriedly. Ronn enters, sees the cake, and tastes it.*)

RONN

>Stale Cake! (*He whistles and waves. Garry and Steven run in to join him. They taste the cake.*)

ALL

>Stale Cake! Come on, you guys! (*Other children enter; all start yelling and run out, following the Stale Cake trail.*)

Scene xiii   The Stale Cake Company at the Railway Station

A train whistle is heard. The members of the Stale Cake Company are standing about with their suitcases resting on the ground, as if waiting on a platform at a railway station. Diana Dumbstrut leans against the match, filing her nails. Daddy Tutti-Fruit Hat sits on his suitcase with his fake moustache pulled up on top of his head. He is picking his teeth. The Electric Piggybank Man, his pig mask pulled up, sits on his luggage between Diana Dumbstrut and Dorothy Doughie. Dorothy Doughie leans against the ladder, smoking. Captain Steal stands behind Dorothy Doughie, and the Oreo Cookie Man stands behind Diana Dumbstrut. Winde lies on the rim, observing everything.

DIANA DUMBSTRUT

What time is it, huh? What time's it supposed to get here? Gee, I'm tired . . . kids've been steppin' all over my boots. Look . . . God, I hate kids.

OREO COOKIE MAN

Yeah . . .

DOROTHY DOUGHIE

How would you like 'em pullin' at your dress all the time, huh? You walk down the street and they tug at your dress. I want a Dorothy Doughie dress, I want a Dorothy Doughie doll! Oh God, teen pukes.

DADDY TUTTI-FRUIT HAT

Hey, that's not a bad idea, sweetheart. A Dorothy Doughie doll, huh?

CAPTAIN STEAL

Right on!

DADDY TUTTI-FRUIT HAT

Dorothy and Don Doughie go camping. (*They ad-lib and laugh.*

Daddy Tutti-Fruit Hat looks at the Oreo Cookie Man.) You've got a little black paint behind your ear, Oreo.

DIANA DUMBSTRUT

Here, I'll get it.

CAPTAIN STEAL

Hey, Diana, do you think I can still pass for thirteen?

DIANA DUMBSTRUT

Sure, kid, you look young.

ELECTRIC PIGGYBANK MAN

We ain't takin' the Dream Wagon. Brakes busted.

DADDY TUTTI-FRUIT HAT

No sweat, Pig, no sweat. The Dream Wagon is junked.

OTHERS

What? Huh? Junked?

DADDY TUTTI-FRUIT HAT

Right! Now it's a spaceship.

OTHERS

Spaceship?

DADDY TUTTI-FRUIT HAT

Reworking the whole organization, see, I've got it all planned out. We're going to call it the Hot Carrot Juice Company. Oreo becomes a new logo! See now, we paint his face orange and give him some green hair and a carrot suit. Mr. Carrot Man! (*The members of the Stale Cake Company ad-lib comments and improvise bits to accompany this routine. Meanwhile Black-Eyed Pea and Bubble steal all the Big Money from their pockets and luggage and strew it across the stage, unseen by the Stale Cake Company. Daddy Tutti-Fruit Hat speaks to Diana Dumbstrut.*) I'll give you a carrot to twirl, sweetheart! You can twirl anything I put in your hand, can't you?

DIANA DUMBSTRUT

(*naively*) Hey, yeah, I could twirl a carrot!

DADDY TUTTI-FRUIT HAT

Peter Rabbit had a human sister, Miss Dorothy Patch! Captain Cabbage. Give me some green stuff, kids. Huh? We'll put some overalls on Pig, Mr. Pig Jeans. We're all set, huh? "Hot Carrot

Juice. Try some on your parents." All right, gimme an A . . . come on, let's try the song. (*The Stale Cake Company sings off-key in the background.*)

> *It's a carrot thing,*
> *It's an artichoke,*
> *It's a rutabaga . . .*

DIANA DUMBSTRUT

What is a rutabaga, anyway? Some kind of *root* or something?

DADDY TUTTI-FRUIT HAT

Oh, come on, I'm starved. Let's go get a Speedy Burger.

OREO COOKIE MAN

Yeah, a good Speedy Burger, huh.

CAPTAIN STEAL

I'm buying. (*He reaches into his pocket for his wallet.*) . . . I'm not buying, where's my money? (*Boogie theme. All begin searching frantically for their money, arguing among themselves and turning on the Electric Piggybank Man. All speak at once: "Where's my money?" "Pig, did you rip off the stash?" "It was right here by my . . ." "I ain't got the money!" "You can't trust anybody any more." The Oreo Cookie Man sees the money lying about; he whistles to the others.*)

OREO COOKIE MAN

It's the money! (*All start grabbing for the money, shouting. They follow the trail of money offstage. Both the trail of money and the trail of cake lead to the Matchbox House. As the lights black out and the Matchbox House slides onstage, Winde is heard singing from where he lies on the rim.*)

WINDE

> *Don't be grabbin' for more than you've got,*
> *Just know that you've got what you need!*
> *Don't be grabbin' for more than you've got,*
> *Just know that you've got what you need!*

Scene xiv   The Big Cookie

Winde, still lying on the rim, observes the Matchbox House people.
Wet Paint Bill and Old Glue Needle are working on umbrellas.
Mother Mary is by the stove, keeping an eye on the Big Cookie.

MOTHER MARY

The Big Cookie's getting brown. (*Black-Eyed Pea and Bubble*
come sliding in, talking excitedly. Wet Paint Bill and Old Glue
Needle light large candles for themselves and Black-Eyed Pea.)

BUBBLE

Mother Mary! Mother Mary! We found out what you meant in
the song.

BLACK-EYED PEA

Yeah! Everybody's coming.

MOTHER MARY

You invited everybody?

BLACK-EYED PEA and BUBBLE

Yeah!

MOTHER MARY

And they're all coming?

BLACK-EYED PEA and BUBBLE

Yeah!

MOTHER MARY

That's fine! OK, get in your places now 'cause the Big Cookie's
gonna be ready in just a minute. Quiet, though, because this is a
holy moment. (*One by one, children and adults arrive at the*
Matchbox House. They enter quietly and gaze in awe at the
house. A spirit of peace and love pervades the group. The children
take seats around the stage and talk softly among themselves as
Mother Mary greets the new arrivals.) Hi! Come on in. Welcome
to the Matchbox House. Welcome! Yes, yes, come in, come on in.
Let me see how the cookie's doin'! Come on in, it'll be ready in a
minute.

292

OLD GLUE NEEDLE

Just sit down and relax. The Big Cookie's comin' out in a minute.

MOTHER MARY

Here comes the Big Cookie! (*She pulls a huge cookie sheet from the oven; on it is an enormous cookie. Everyone "ooohs" and "aahs." They pass the cookie around, each breaking off a piece, sharing in the communion.*) Pass it on around! This ain't no stale cake either, just good fresh cookie.

SHEILA

How much?

MOTHER MARY

It's free. Here. I saw ya all on the street before, so you're welcome here at the Matchbox House.

BUBBLE

Hi, guys!

ALL

Hi, Bubble!

WET PAINT BILL

(*points to one boy*) I knew you'd be here. I saw your face in the street! Ha, ha, ha, ha!

BLACK-EYED PEA

I'll show you how to make that birdhouse tomorrow, all right?

BUBBLE

Have you seen my flute? I can teach you how to make one exactly like it.

BLACK-EYED PEA

You'll have to come back tomorrow. I know you like kittens, and I'll have some tomorrow. (*Percussion. The members of the Stale Cake Company enter down the slide one by one, each entrance accented by a rim shot on a drum in the orchestra. They gather in a clump upstage. They growl at the Cookie Land people, who growl back at them.*)

WET PAINT BILL

Oh, come on in, but don't you fret. Your cake may be stale, but ours ain't. (*The Stale Cake Company growls again, but the Matchbox House people growl back and frighten them.*)

DIANA DUMBSTRUT

Let's get out of here!

DOROTHY DOUGHIE

Help!

OREO COOKIE MAN

We gives up! We gives up!

DADDY TUTTI-FRUIT HAT

But we're trapped!

MOTHER MARY

Oh, no, folks, never mind. Everybody's welcome here in the Matchbox House. But only if you're joinin' in with us, only if you're sharin'.

DADDY TUTTI-FRUIT HAT

Oh, yeah? How much does it cost?

CAPTAIN STEAL

How much does it cost to join your club?

MOTHER MARY

No, no, no, not money! You don't pay to be filled with the spirit. You don't pay! You share in the spirit. You can't buy it, you gotta know it!

ELECTRIC PIGGYBANK MAN

We never took nothin' we didn't pay for!

OLD GLUE NEEDLE

That's 'cause you forgot the first recipe the good Lord ever gave ya.

WET PAINT BILL

You can't tell the difference between a piece of stale cake and a worn-out old shoe.

OLD GLUE NEEDLE

You probably never mixed a real recipe that makes a real cookie before in your life.

MOTHER MARY

You sell aprons, but I bet you never wore one and got it dirty in the kitchen. Here, taste this good fresh cookie. (*She gives the Stale Cake Company people some of the Big Cookie.*)

STALE CAKE COMPANY

Uhmmmmm! Uhmmmmm!

MOTHER MARY

Don't be greedy now! Now before you can join in and share, you got to do some work and make a real recipe, 'fore you can join us.

WET PAINT BILL

That's your penance for sellin' stuff nobody needs and gettin', gettin', gettin'! Take off that hair and all; it might fall in the mixing bowl and you know that ain't no good!

OLD GLUE NEEDLE

And all that stuff you're wearin' ain't no good neither!

MOTHER MARY

Now get goin' and do some good doin'. If you don't, you're goin' to be starvin', and whatever you do . . . (*gesturing for everyone to join her*) give, give, give! And remember, my friends . . .

MATCHBOX HOUSE PEOPLE

(*speaking one after another*) If you're cold! Hungry! Crabby! Frightened! Lost!

MOTHER MARY

You've just got to put it all together in one big bowl!

WET PAINT BILL

Now hurry up and get mixin'!

BLACK-EYED PEA

Get cookin'!

OLD GLUE NEEDLE

And get bakin'!

MOTHER MARY

The love in this here Matchbox House is yours for the takin'! (*The Stale Cake Company exits. Theme: "Put It All Together into One Big Bowl!"* Mother Mary sings.*)

Oh, put it all together into one big bowl!
Mix a new batch of cookies, now you been told!
You'll never be hungry now in one big bowl!
Put it all together into one big bowl!

*Music on pages 304 and 305.

(*Mother Mary sings the chorus, and the others onstage sing an echo-and-counterpoint.*)

MOTHER MARY	ALL
You've got to put it . . .	*Put it!*
All together!	*'Gether!*
You've got to put it . . .	*Put it!*
All together!	*'Gether!*
You've got to put it . . .	*Put it!*
All together!	*All together!*
You've got to put it all to-	*Put — it — all —*
gether into one big bowl!	*in — one big bowl!*

(*Mother Mary sings the next verse.*)

> *Oh, put it all together into one big bowl!*
> *This recipe works for young and old!*
> *You're gonna get the spirit now in one big bowl!*
> *Put it all together into one big bowl!*

(*Mother Mary and the others repeat the echo-and-counterpoint chorus as before. Then Mother Mary sings the next verse.*)

> *Oh, put it all together into one big bowl!*
> *Pinch of yours, some of mine, you don't need gold!*
> *Guaranteed to taste delicious from one big bowl!*
> *Put it all together into one big bowl!*

(*Mother Mary and the others repeat the chorus again. The members of the Stale Cake Company return without makeup or wigs, wearing chef suits and hats and carrying utensils. They set up a small table and mix a batch of dough as the others sing. Those who are seated get up, one by one, as the spirit builds; led by Black-Eyed Pea, they dance and sing down the center aisle, passing out cookies. The members of the Stale Cake Company follow the rest, passing out cookies and lemonade in tin cups. The audience is clapping and singing. The cast goes to the back of the house, around the sides, and back onto the stage for the finish of the song, urging people from the audience to join them. The house lights come up, and the people in the cast mix and visit with the people in the audience, again inviting them onto the stage. The spirit of communion pervades the final scene.*)

Production History

The Cookie Jar was first produced at the Minneapolis Institute of Arts by the Children's Theatre Company of the Minneapolis Society of Fine Arts on March 4, 1972. The script was edited by Linda Walsh Jenkins with the assistance of Carol K. Metz.

Original Cast

Bubble .... John Newcombe
Bubble (understudy) .... Joe Paatalo
Winde .... Ken Williams
Black-Eyed Pea .... Kim Livingston
Old Glue Needle .... John Jenkins
Wet Paint Bill .... Bill Dovali
Mother Mary .... Josephine Brown
Daddy Tutti-Fruit Hat .... Guy Paul
Diana Dumbstrut .... Wendy Lehr
Dorothy Doughie .... Barbara Larsen
Oreo Cookie Man .... Jim Stowell
Captain Steal .... Christian Mulkey
Electric Piggybank Man .... Pat McNellis
People of Cookie Land:
 Tory Bailey, Sue Batchelor, Matt Brassil, David Campbell, Nance Campbell, David Draper, Barry Goldman, Kim Hines, John Kadulski, Kathy Kennedy, Laurel Kennedy, Kevin King, Garry Lewis, Frank McGovern, Bridget McNellis, Susie Peterson, David Pichette, Mary Ann Raymond, Steven Rydberg, Kathy Sullivan, Ginni Swanson, Artie Thompson, Audrey Thompson, Victor Walter

Directed and produced by John Clark Donahue
Music composed by Roberta Carlson
Set design by Jon Barkla
Costume design by Gene Buck
Properties by Patricia O'Leary
Lighting by Jon Baker

"All right! We've got your number, sweetheart!" (Photograph by Richard Paulaha.)

"Black-Eyed Pea, Black-Eyed Pea, if you're wonderin' where this song comes from, then take a look at me!" (Photograph by Richard Paulaha.)

"Miss Diana Dumbstrut, the Girl with the Golden Goose!" (Photograph by Richard Paulaha.)

"And written in flour under the sink was this message: 'Bake a cookie for me!'" (Photograph by Gary Sherman.)

Sweet Jesus, Precious Savior

Black-Eyed Pea

NOTE: Music for *The Cookie Jar* composed by Roberta Carlson.
Copyright © 1974 by Roberta Carlson. All rights reserved.

Old Glue Needle and Wet Paint Bill

Get, Get, Get!

Moderato – Swing Tempo

Ya got-ta get, get, get; Ya got-ta get, get, get; When the

world's in trou-ble and you don't know what to do, ya got-ta get, get, get.

Put It All Together into One Big Bowl!

put it____ all to-geth-er,___ You've got to

put it____ all to-geth-er, You've got to

put it____ all to-geth-er, You've got to

put it all to-geth-er in-to one big bowl.